John Henry W. Stuckenberg

The Final Science

Spiritual materialism

John Henry W. Stuckenberg

The Final Science
Spiritual materialism

ISBN/EAN: 9783337332266

Printed in Europe, USA, Canada, Australia, Japan

Cover: Foto ©Andreas Hilbeck / pixelio.de

More available books at **www.hansebooks.com**

OR

SPIRITUAL MATERIALISM.

BEING A STRICT APPLICATION OF THE MOST APPROVED
MODERN SCIENTIFIC PRINCIPLES TO THE SOLUTION
OF THE DEEPEST PROBLEMS
OF THE AGE.

FUNK & WAGNALLS.

NEW YORK: 1885.   LONDON:
10 AND 12 DEY STREET.   44 FLEET STREET.

CONTENTS.

THE FINAL SCIENCE.

CHAPTER I.

THE CRISIS IN MATERIALISM.

" Hear, Nature, hear ;
Dear Goddess, hear !"
LEAR.

By far the most interesting portions of history are
the world's crises in thought. To the ordinary reader
they may be less striking than political revolutions ;
but the thinker finds them of transcendent importance,
because he sees in them the seeds whence all the
variety and beauty which appear on the pages of history have sprung. The results are apparent to all, the
causes are hid ; but the discovery of these hidden
sources of the stream of human events makes history
valuable to the student and worthy of the philosopher's attention.

What is true of history applies also to the study of
the present. Much as the mind may ordinarily be
engrossed by the infinite diversity and ceaseless, fever-
ish activity in social and national life, in its deeper
moods it will seek the principles, the underlying
thought, the motives and aims, which are the causes
and commentaries of the phenomena. Only by com-

prehending its spirit can we understand the age itself
—a spirit deep and subtle, the product of the entire
development of the past, of whose thoughts, disputes,
problems, and results it is the heir.   The causes, ap-
parently infinite in number and variety, and extremely
intricate, are a skein whose tangles are increased by
the attempt to unravel them.   Sharp conflicts, the
rapid change of opinions, together with the feeling of
uncertainty and expectancy, indicate that we are passing through a crisis and are approaching an epoch
which will inaugurate a new era.   The revolution in
thought which is now in progress does not affect social
and political questions merely, but also those fundamental principles which involve all thought and emotion—the whole life and every human interest.   The
crisis does not consist in the originality of the problems demanding solution, for they are as old as philosophic thought, but in the fact that these problems,
which formerly occupied the attention of a few minds,
have now become universal and are recognized as
vital.   The solution cannot be deferred as in former
times, for now life and thought, to say nothing of the
heart, depend on it.

By tracing the phenomena of individual and national
life to their causes, and these causes to the ultimate
problem lying behind them and at the basis of all
thought and being, we come to the question of materialism.   In the search for the cause of things, which
is the mind's *ultima Thule?*   What substance must
be regarded as first, and therefore as the seed of the
universe ?   What is that eternal Something, of which
the temporal is but a manifestation ?   Matter ?   Spirit ?
Matter and Spirit ?   Something behind both and from

which they have sprung, neither Matter nor Spirit, but their Creator? Or is there in reality neither Matter nor Spirit, but only an agnostic Cause of the phenomena erroneously assigned by us to body and mind?

After spending many years in profoundly investigating this problem, I have at last struck bottom. Unhesitatingly and unconditionally I adopt materialism, and declare it to be the sole and all-sufficient explanation of the universe. This affords the only thoroughly scientific system; and nowhere but in its legitimate conclusions can thought find a suitable resting-place, the heart complete satisfaction, and life a perfect basis. Unless it accepts this system, philosophy will be but drift-wood, instead of the stream of thought whose current bears all truth. Materialism, thorough, consistent, and fearless, not the timid, reserved, and half-hearted kind, is the hope of the world. When it attains the goal toward which it presses, there will be a revolution whose far-reaching consequences are unparalleled. Copernicus taught that the sun is the centre around which the planets revolve; Kant made the mind the centre and source of thought, so that all objects of investigation must adapt themselves to its nature; but materialism proposes a grander revolution, since it goes deeper and has loftier aims than Copernicus or Kant. Instead of resting content with petty inquiries respecting the centre of the solar system and mental phenomena, it penetrates to the centre and substance of all thought and phenomena, and of all real and possible existence. Not only does it settle all questions proposed by philosophy heretofore, but also the deepest problems which can

occur to the mind ; and the solution which materialism gives justifies its claim to be the Final Science,
the Ultimate Philosophy, and the Last Thought.

Those who have never passed beyond the border-
land of this sublime system can form no conception
of its beneficence, while those wholly outside of its
territory are, in their ignorance, apt to abuse this intellectual saviour of the world.   To appreciate its be-
nign influences one must pass through it, following
its principles to their utmost consequences ; he must,
like the author, lose his mind and heart in its contem-
plation and enjoyment.   After this experimental test
he can safely recommend it as the redemptive power of
mankind.   He knows that it only needs a fair chance in
order to change radically the thoughts, interests, and
pursuits of humanity ; to confer favors on individuals
and society which the most vivid imagination has failed
to picture ; to transform science, literature, morals, religion, and politics ; and to make real in this life that
heaven of which religious enthusiasts have only
dreamt.   After its reign becomes universal, materialism will convert barbarism into enlightenment, vul-
garity into refinement, ignorance into culture, and
superstition into science.   It will promote only material interests, and will so develop man that he must
find in them perfect satisfaction.   Long ago it established the truth that "a man is what he eats ;" and
in the blessed era of its supremacy the meat and drink
of men will be selected with special reference to the
production of virtue, refinement, and scholarship.
Since national life depends mainly on soil, climate,
and other material causes, these will be cultivated ex-
clusively, intellect always being able to take care of

itself. Political institutions will be so arranged that
·a change of diet will convert criminals into saints, and
dunces into scientists. All knowledge respecting
man, as anthropology, psychology, sociology, political
economy, and ethics, will be reduced to physical science ; and man, animals, vegetables, and inorganic
matter being brought within the province of physics
and chemistry, will form a scientific unity such as
thought demands, but has never been able to establish on account of idealistic and spiritualistic excres-
cences.

Every profound scholar and friend of humanity who
passes through materialism, and makes it part of himself—mastering it fully and being completely mas-
tered by it—recognizes in it the desire of the nations,
and the fulfilment of man's brightest hopes. Intent
on promoting its speedy victory, the author recently
visited the continent of Europe to study its progress,
hoping to gather such facts and arguments as would
banish still existing remnants of spiritualism from
philosophy, literature, and life. He, however, returned saddened and discouraged by the result of his
pilgrimage. Much was expected from Germany,
which has been so prominent in spreading the evangel
of materialism ; but it soon became evident that in
that country this system is passing through a fearful
crisis, and is in danger of losing its grip on educated
men. There are in the universities professors on whom
great hopes were once centred, who now turn their
backs upon it ; and in recent works on science, philosophy, and literature, it is frequently discussed in a
spirit which savors strongly of contempt. Recently
a literary article, which was not written in the interest

of religion, declared, with a malicious air of triumph,
that materialism had been scientifically overthrown.
The last work on the omnipotence and omnipresence
of matter is crass and consistent enough to give it the
stamp of orthodoxy. It closes with a poem contain-
ing this sentiment addressed to the reader : " Matter
alone reigns eternally in nature, and, as an intellectual
power, becomes conscious in thee." The leading philosophical journal of Germany disposes of the work
with this single remark : " This standpoint has long
ago been overthrown !" Since the deepest German
works are not adapted to the popular taste, books like
this might be translated and circulated so as to make
the impression that the leading thinkers of that land
favor materialism. Clear, refined, exact, and profound as this peerless system is, it is not advisable to
let it be known that continental scholars speak of it as
crude, shallow, and immature, and that they do not
blush to treat the best product of the ages as a mere
chaos of opinions. The marvel is that " The History
of Materialism," by Lange, which ought to have
helped our cause, dealt it a blow which made it stag-
ger. Like the bird of wisdom, materialism sees best
at night, and then appears to finest advantage. But
scholars have ruthlessly dragged it out of its sphere
into the sunlight, and have not merely looked at it,
but through it ; as a consequence, the respect which
mystery inspires has vanished. It has come to such a
pass in Germany, that those who follow materialism
unconditionally to its ultimate conclusions run the risk
of being laughed at as charlatans and pitied as fools !
The scholars of the land of Bismarck and Moltke are
unwilling to plant themselves firmly on our solid base,

and they may again fall into one of their mystical, metaphysical, idealistic fits.

We materialists, who are more attached to stuff than to intangible ideas, may not fully appreciate the danger of our beloved system in the land where some of its stanchest adherents have flourished. In spite of the great revival in material interests, that nation has too many ideas and ideals, which are incompatible with our philosophy. Somehow, the assumptions and conclusions and tendencies of even the most refined materialists seem to have produced a surfeit of good things, and we see men turn with loathing from the only system which is the panacea for all ills. Kant, that old transcendental idealist, is again studied with enthusiasm, and the merciless criticism of his philosophy is applied to our naïve surmises. The modern idealist, Lotze, is also gaining ground. Stern logicians like Sigwart actually recognize an immaterial deity! Scientists speak less confidently about their knowledge of matter, and now admit that there are many things for which none of its known properties and laws can account. Ulrici's works are but few among the many which create the suspicion that materialists assume too much and prove too little. And now from Dorpat there comes a volume (by Teichmueller) declaring that the real world of matter is only phenomenal; it puts mind on the throne of the universe, and permits a personal God to usurp the place of the atoms; and this volume is only the forerunner of a whole system which threatens to abuse materialism, and to prove it a vulgar dirt-philosophy! Nor do the works on psychology, logic, theory of knowledge, and ethics inspire any hope. Even physiolo-

gists, who are so much indebted to matter, fail to see
it after they have lost sight of its properties.

This is not all. There are German scientists of
eminence who, in spite of their liberal education, persist in devoting themselves strictly and severely to a
specialty, as if they were its slaves. It is self-evident
that such scholars have not the breadth of materialism ; they cannot be prepared, like those who over-
look all the sciences, to indorse its generous assertions.
Helmholtz, for instance, spends day after day in his
laboratory, trying to solve the problems of light, heat,
and electricity ; and when he lectures on these subjects, he confines himself so narrowly to them that he
does not use, even for illustration, the cognate
branches of metaphysics, ethics, and religion. Yet he
is looked upon as a scientist ! The fact is, that many
of his countrymen have no other notion of science
than that it is mathematically exact : that it is limited
to facts and their laws, and does not reach down into
the substances themselves ; that its hypotheses require
demonstration before they cease to be hypotheses ; that
the laws must be drawn from the facts, not the facts
from the laws ; that the facts must be found, not invented, however much they may be needed ; and that
a scientist is not necessarily an authority outside of his
specialty, but scientific only so far as he deals mathematically with what is exact and submits to mathematical tests. These bondmen have no idea how much
science they lose by eternally experimenting and painfully noting the results. Instead of burying themselves in laboratory and study, they might have standing and influence with the scientific masses if they cultivated more of the poetry and less of the dryness of

science. Materialism has nothing to hope from investigators afraid to launch out and pass over the whole surface of the sea of science, and willing to make only such contributions as result from tedious demonstrations.

Even Du Bois-Reymond, who appreciates the flowers of rhetoric and understands the art of seizing the occasion to give flings at religion, speaks with contempt of those who leave the severe methods of science and put their fancy to the solution of physical problems. Virchow is a politician as well as a scientist; and yet so little reverence has he for the savants who have enriched science with metaphysical speculations and poetic facts, that he administers to them the most scathing rebukes. These and the other scientific plodders warn earnestly against the deductive method which has of late became so fashionable; and with a contempt not even disguised they speak of the popular philosophers who invent and spread beautiful theories without stopping to prove them; and they absurdly find fault with creative minds which promote science with their instincts, intuitions, and *à priori* conclusions. Their language leads to the inference that they prefer to leave the riddles of nature unsolved rather than admit guesses at truth into science. Wundt, in his Logic, gives the methodology of all the sciences; but how he enslaves the liberal spirit by his rigorous mathematics! Thumb-screws belong to the Middle Ages, not to the free nineteenth century. Of course such toilers and enslavers lack the progressive modern scientific spirit; and if they prevail, we may as soon expect the return of the dark ages as the triumph of materialism. While a poetic scientist easily and for-

ever settles the most momentous questions and then
spreads his wings for new flights, these delvers do not
budge, but slowly and patiently examine and re-
examine facts, test the conclusions drawn from them,
and instead of making any advance they find at last that
what was long ago settled finally is not settled at all.
Even if a theory explains all the facts, they hesitate
to accept it under the flimsy pretext that a hundred
other theories might do the same, and all cannot be
true ! This proves that they are plodding in inductive
grooves and hopelessly sticking in scientific ruts.
Now, when such men ridicule the assumptions of materialism we know how to estimate their opinions ; and
when they attempt to bring their arguments to bear on
us, we can easily shift our light artillery before they
get their heavy batteries into position.

Still, the outlook in Germany is not without hope ;
faithful adherents of our system may still be found.
Young medical students who for the first time dissect
a corpse are startled in not finding the soul which has
fled, and thus they receive mighty materialistic inspiration. If the soul had been spiritual it would not
have fled, but would have remained in the body, where
it could easily have been seen. Therefore the fact that
it has fled, or, if still in the body, is invisible, is conclusive proof that the soul is a material substance.
Fortunately, there are also physicians, professors, and
authors who are materialists, but they are more modest
and less noisy than formerly. But the stanchest adherents of our Final Philosophy are found among the
laity, who devote themselves heartily to material interests. They have faithful brethren and co-laborers
in Russia, France, Belgium, and other States, who at

the risk of martyrdom make themselves the terror of
idealists and spiritualists, as well as of monarchs.
Happily the thorough and influential materialists of
Germany are popular rather than profound, and for
some time they will likely conserve the basis of materialism found in the scientific masses. On the principle of the survival of the fittest, they will outlive
our more reserved brethren. They deserve to be rec-
ommended as models and as authorities of great significance in their special line.

Without intending any invidious distinctions, we
can point to Moleschott, Vogt, Büchner, and Haeckel
as heroic defenders of materialistic faith, whose opinions may be accepted as orthodox, scientific dogmas.
Ignoring whatever laborious researches they may have
made, amateurs and all who are unable to investigate
for themselves can take the convictions of these men
and make them the basis of their science. Those who
have time and inclination to make researches may
not want to follow the speculations of these natural
philosophers, nor is it necessary. Their value to our
cause does not consist in their investigations, but in
their conclusions. Since they start and end with
these, it is sufficient if they are adopted ; what is
thrown in between is merely intended to fill up, and
may be omitted as not essential to the argument. If
the deductions with which these authors begin are accepted, the whole matter is settled finally, and to
bring proof after that is like dipping water into the
sea.

The last three of these leaders are already known
to American and English materialists, but not so thoroughly as they deserve to be. My deep indebtedness

to them impels me to promote their popularity in
America and Great Britain.   This work bears numerous traces of my dependence on their authority ; and
as they are acquiring valuable experience in the crisis
of materialism in Germany, they may give us material
aid when we pass through the fire.   They have this
enormous advantage : religious scruples and moral
prejudices have not the slightest effect on their materialistic hypotheses ; so free are they from all bias
that their writings reveal a wholesome dread of religion and a holy horror of the supernatural.   They
are as familiar as Mr. Herbert Spencer with the Unknowable, and have conveniently converted it into
Matter, Force, and Laws.   If only the faith of these
heroes could be made contagious !   To Vogt and
Büchner it is so evident that there is nothing supersensible, that it is a mark of folly to inquire whether
there is anything besides matter.   There is nothing
finical about them ; they are not afraid of soiling their
polished boots, but are the genuine, heroic sort of materialists, with a deep affection for matter, so that they
recognize it as their affinity, and are ready to wade
through it and to lie down in it.

Professor Carl Vogt is brilliant—a diamond, but
seen only in the rough.   Exquisite refinement must
not be expected when he tackles mental phenomena.
The mind is evidently not his sphere ; the grossness
of the material he usually handles serves as an apology
for his occasional and semi-occasional coarseness.
Those who swear by him, however, do not need this
apology.   I have found it best to take his deductions
at his own estimate, since it adds marvellously to their
conclusiveness.   Generally his arguments are light

and his influences so easily drawn that it is a delight to follow him. The facts for which he cannot frame a satisfactory hypothesis are not worthy of being obtruded on a credulous, scientific public. He has a trick of interspersing his mathematical reasoning with fierce attacks on his opponents ; and it is at times hard to discover whether his science exists for the sake of the attacks, or the attacks for the sake of the science. His fury does not, however, affect the easy flow of his argument, but is often its most effective part. Frequently he illustrates the truth that there may be awful wrath in celestial minds. Will Jupiter stoop to argue when he can strike his foe with a thunderbolt ? Mr. Vogt is an authority on the morality and religion of brutes, and I shall quote some choice gems from him on these subjects.

Büchner's " Kraft und Stoff " lies at my side, and I cherish it as the materialistic Bible. The weary, thirsty pilgrim never turns to it in vain for refreshment. As it is pre-eminently a popular work, not spoiled by the dullness of science, it is admirably adapted to the masses as their scientific gospel. The preface to the first edition has this motto from Boz : " Now what I want is facts." I, too, feel that this is what he wants ; but the lack is amply compensated for by hypotheses and emphatic assertions. The essence of the book is condensed in the author's second sentence : " No force without matter—no matter without force." He who accepts this inspired declaration, and at the same time assumes with the author that there is nothing in the universe but matter and its force, can afford to lay aside this sacred volume ; all that remains is only the shell for this precious kernel.

Professor Haeckel closes this series of illustrious names. He deserves the more attention because Mr. Darwin esteemed him highly as a disciple, and because on some points the disciple became leader, and the master follower. This author wrote, among other things, a romance on the " History of Creation," of which Mr. Darwin says that in it " he fully discusses the genealogy of man." Yes, rather fully, connecting the banks of great gaps by links of fancy. So successful is he as a creator, that he has forever exploded the old dictum—from nothing, nothing comes. But his gigantic efforts do not receive that scientific appreciation at home which they deserve ; it therefore behooves our materialists to rally to his support. In spite of his enormous labor to trace the history of creation, that book is treated in his own country as if the events recorded had occurred nowhere except in the brain of its author ! But his genealogy of man is really of immense materialistic value, since it traces the descent of man through the entire animal creation to the gorilla. Between the gorilla and man a link is wanting, which Mr. Haeckel generously supplies—a charity for which apes and men should be grateful. He shoves in a human ape just where absolutely necessary to save the genealogical table—a fashionable method of meeting the exigencies of hypotheses. This author sets a commendable example in bridging unfordable streams. And for such invaluable service to science he is ridiculed, his hypotheses are pronounced " fancies," and occasionally terms still less dignified and not so scientific are applied to them. Du Bois-Reymond says unceremoniously : " These genealogical tables, which are the product of an artificial fancy working with unfettered presumption, rather than of a fancy scientifically disciplined, are worth about as much as the genealogical tables of the Homeric heroes.   If I want to read romances, I know of something better than the ' History of Creation.' " After Mr. Darwin's hearty praise of the book in his " Descent of Man," it is sacrilegious to speak of it so irreverently.*

Similar utterances have become so common in Germany, that in intellectual circles our beloved materialism, together with the inspiration of its prophets and apostles, is losing caste.   Keenly feeling the contumely with which our fathers and brethren are treated, I recognized it as a solemn duty to Matter to make an earnest appeal to my co-laborers to be true to the sublime principles of our philosophy, and to conserve its blessed fruits.   Our esteemed German helpers, who are becoming the laughing-stock even of infidel scientists in their own country, might be taken into our bosom, and welcomed to our free soil with socialists and others who find it advisable to forsake their native land.   Their translated works are already spreading supernal blessings among our people.   If more of their works and a few of the authors were imported, it would aid us in getting rid of our excess of morality and superfluity of religion.   This devout consummation is one of the aims of my book, whose frequent reference to these writers is calculated to

---

* In the introduction Mr. Darwin refers to Vogt, Büchner, and Haeckel. They evidently had much influence on him, especially the last, of whose book on the " History of Creation" he says : " If this work had appeared before my essay had been written, I should probably never have completed it."

promote their healthy views among us. With a
judicious culture of their spirit we might make our
hospitable shores the eternal home of materialism.

We have special advantages for the culture of this
system. If in the land where it recently flourished so
luxuriantly, materialism, like a certain bird, buries its
head, there is still enough left for those who hanker
after such things ; and it is not the head which charms
them. By sedulously avoiding those pursuits which
have endangered the divinity of matter abroad, we
can firmly establish its throne and secure its reign.
There are certain notions which dissolve the rocks on
which it rests into quicksands ; they must accordingly
be shunned as dangerous. Thus where the German
philosophers cultivate the reason, let our philosophic
giants cultivate sensation ; while their minds work according to fixed laws which evolve the categories of
thought, let our great minds be blank sheets of paper,
passively receiving impressions from things ; where
they have ideas which are Platonic and remind one of
the war between Nominalists and Realists, let our
thinkers produce systems in which ideas are simply
the representations of outward objects, and it will soon
become evident that our purely sensualistic philosophy furnishes a sufficiently solid basis for materialism.

Unfortunately, we too have men of scientific influence who lack the materialistic spirit. Ascribing to
matter certain well-known properties, they hesitate to
affirm its existence where they fail to find these. In
such cases a thorough materialist has the courage to
swear that there is matter and nothing but matter, and
is skilful enough to adapt the properties to the exigencies of the case, or to let them shift for themselves.

Some of our reputed scholars, however, lack this scientific heroism and skill, and still cherish the exploded notion that in science demonstration must precede conviction. They limit science too much, robbing it of breadth and freedom in the interest of depth and thoroughness. They do not appreciate easy victories. Materialism has nothing to hope from men who limit their possessions to the territory which they have actually conquered.

It was mortifying beyond expression to hear Professor Allman, in his presidential address before the British Association some years ago, say : " Between thought and the physical phenomena of matter there is not only no analogy, but no conceivable analogy. . . . The chasm between unconscious life and thought is deep and impassable, and no transitional phenomena can be found by which, as a bridge, we may span it over." True ; but we materialists do not profess to bridge the chasm ; we simply fill it with matter and walk over. This overcomes all difficulty. Even Professor Tyndall, from whom we receive so much support, and whose utterances at times rise to the sublimity of materialism, occasionally gives us a slap. Thus he says : " The passage from the physics of the brain to the corresponding facts of consciousness is unthinkable." Well, suppose it is ; we do not claim it as thinkable, but simply as a fact. Quite unnecessarily he adds : " Were our minds and senses so expanded, strengthened, and illuminated as to enable us to see and feel the very molecules of the brain—were we capable of following all their motions, all their groupings, all their electrical discharges, if there be such, and were we intimately acquainted with the corresponding states of thought and feeling, we should probably be as far as ever from the solution of the problem, How are these physical processes connected with the facts of consciousness? The chasm between the two classes of phenomena would still remain intellectually impassable." Yes, "intellectually impassable," but not materially! How is it if you dump matter into the chasm? This shows how easily such arguments against materialism can be upset.

Professor Huxley has been of service to us; but when we expect most from him he forsakes us utterly. No words can express our indebtedness to Mr. Herbert Spencer; yet the materialistic flavor of his utterances depends chiefly on the stage of the evolution in which they are expressed. If Professors Tait, Balfour Stewart, William Thomson, and others who tread in their footsteps have been of any service to materialism, I am not aware of the fact. It is probable that they will never earn our gratitude. If they are mentioned at all in this volume, it is only for the sake of warning our fraternity against them.

Those who in science prefer mathematics to a creative imagination should not be blamed for their taste; they deserve no more censure than Newton for not having all the wisdom of our modern natural philosophers. They are not, however, the heroes of this volume. It glories in the popular scientist who frees himself from the drudgery of induction. He is versatile, speaking as glibly of religion as of science, and being an equal authority in both; he uses the gems of poetry, the flowers of rhetoric, and the thrill of eloquence to increase the depth of his science; and he experiences not the slightest difficulty in bringing his profoundest thought within easy appreciation of popular audiences. This kind of science has already become hereditary on our shores. Its nature is such that it is also readily spread by contagion. If one original voice proclaims it, there will be a thousand echoes. The facility with which it is transmitted is its best recommendation. Our school boys can fathom it ; even the brain of a fashionable young lady has room enough for it ; our editors have it at their fingers' ends ; we have critics who are such masters of it that they dispose of scientific works without the trouble of reading them ; glib lecturers have the art of turning its conclusions into coin ; negro minstrels give point to their jokes with its profundity ; our novels get a learned air by hints at it ; politicians make it their recreation ; ministers occasionally spice their sermons with it ; the upper ten make it the attraction of their drawing-rooms, and the lower millions are inspired by its materialistic ideals. We can afford to glory in that popular science which lights our streets, runs our machinery, propels our steamers, ennobles our cheap literature, utilizes our morals, and dispenses with religion. We can boast of novices with scientific instincts, who know more intuitively than Galileo could discover from the swinging of a lamp, or Newton from the fall of an apple ; who are exempt from laborious experiments, profound thoughts, and mathematical calculations ; who solve without thought problems which scientists of other ages left unsolved after the most thorough investigation ; and we are blessed with authors to whom it is mere sport to dispose of subjects which Aristotle, Descartes, Leibnitz, and Kant found too difficult. We have scientific

giants who are peers of the grossest materialists on the
continent of Europe.

These are our patron saints, on whom we shall depend if ever our blessed materialism is doomed to pass
through a crisis ; they will help to secure the victory
of Matter over mind, and to make it popular as well
as universal. Popular materialism, firmly rooted in a
faith which need not give a reason for itself, is the
safest and most rational. Let it be introduced into the
hearts of the masses ! Somehow it meets with serious
obstacles from men whose perverted philosophy is not
satisfied with the appearance, but irrationally demands
an explanation of things. Those given to the mental
handling of phenomena are not prepared to appreciate our postulates ; and when they follow our reasoning they fail to reach our conclusions. The man who
does not cheerfully grant that mind is Matter, and
that thought is a purely physical and chemical product, has not the stuff of which materialists are made.
Materialism needs scholars who are liberal enough to
confer on Matter all it needs to accomplish whatever
occurs. If these cannot be found at Johns Hopkins,
Yale, Harvard, Oxford, and Cambridge, let them be
sought among the unperverted and unbiassed masses.
No false training unfits them to receive our principles
and adopt our conclusions, while there is much in our
spirit which will allure them. We only need fearless
statements, backed by a conviction which is equal to a
demonstration ; arguments can also be used when convenient. There are minds to which materialism naturally commends itself, and over these it exerts a magi-
cal power. The press and platform must also be
enlisted more zealously in our favor. Such progress

may then be expected that all " spiritual whoredom" will cease ; and morals and religion will no longer weigh like an incubus on the hearts of the people. Even outward respect for priests, for fetid traditions, and rotten superstitions will cease when we unfurl our true colors. The time will soon come when materialism can safely throw aside its mask and fearlessly draw its logical inferences. Some cowards may shrink back in horror, but multitudes, especially in our great cities, will hail it as the harbinger of a carnival, such as their hearts have long coveted.

The recent discussions of materialism seem to indicate that a crisis also awaits it in our land and England. Not only theologians, but also philosophers and scientists are beginning to test its quality. Whether it can stand inspection here any better than on the Continent will depend somewhat on the inspectors. This volume is calculated to be a bulwark of materialistic philosophy in the coming crisis, and may be regarded as an unqualified authority on final science. Those who are so fortunate as to catch the spirit of this work, which it has caught from the materialists of the day, will become the scientists of the future. Those philosophers who can take a particle of dirt and from it evolve all mind and thought—who can put the atoms through the evolutions and involutions necessary to construct the universe, and who can develop the ape into man, are the favorites of this scientific volume.

If the crisis becomes severe, it may be found expedient to change our system so as to meet emergencies. The term *Spiritual Materialism*, if generally adopted to designate our philosophy, might overcome some of the prejudices against us. The change of name, of course, does not imply a change of base. "Spiritual" might relieve our science of that suspicion of coarseness which prevents its influence over certain minds.

The following Principles have been selected with scrupulous care from works on materialism, and from such as prepare the way for it. If any one questions the genuineness of these Principles, I simply refer him to the literature on the subject. My original intention of giving the scientific authorities for each Principle had to be abandoned ; their number being legion, all could not have been mentioned, and those omitted would have felt themselves slighted. In our own brotherhood, the Principles will at once be heartily acknowledged ; and every student of our philosophy knows that they are the foundation-stones on which materialists, though sometimes unconsciously, build their superstructure.

Since writing the above I have attended the meetings of the British Association at Montreal and of the American, at Philadelphia. To my amazement I found that during the respective Sundays prayer-meetings were held by members ! On inquiring into these strange proceedings, I learned that they were of long standing in the British Association, while the American scientists instituted the practice four or five years ago. Just as if Tyndall had not settled such things with his prayer-test ! This outrage on ordinary intelligence and scientific propriety is another argument for the zealous promotion of uncompromising materialism.

CHAPTER II.

First First Principle. The Basis of Science.

" We must take things as they really are, not as we think them." —VIRCHOW.

SPIRITUAL Materialism, or the Final and Absolute Science, rests squarely on nature. Lying behind all other thought as the foundation of all thinking, it might be called the *base* science. It takes for granted only so much as it needs to get along comfortably, and all its assumptions, surmises, and conjectures are self-evident. Besides these postulates, it also picks up the facts lying about loosely on the surface of things, and puts them where most needed. The materialist takes them for what they are worth to him, and rationally banishes from his science all such silly questions as : Where did I get these facts ? Do they represent states of the mind or things external ? What is the relation of my conception to reality ? Being stubborn things, he never questions facts, but simply takes them as they are given. Metaphysical fools may claim that we know things only as they affect our minds, and that

---

* In order to avoid the charge of plagiarism, I think it best to admit candidly that for the subject of this chapter and some of its inspiration I am indebted to the first volume of the " Synthetic Philosophy."

all knowledge is but a revelation of the states of consciousness ; and it may be that this is the case with
metaphysicians.   With materialists it is otherwise.
Nature being their element and familiarity with it
their forte, it is not their mission to know anything of
mental phenomena except that they are vague, unre-
liable, and purely material.   Thoughtfully they avoid
brooding over mind, for "that way madness lies."
Intent only on exact observation, they never "with
inspection nice" enter

> "The mystic labyrinths of the mind,
> Where thought, of notice ever shy, behind
> Thought, disappearing, still retired ; and still,
> Thought meeting thought, and thought awakening thought,
> And mingling still with thought in endless maze,
> Bewildered observation."

The advanced materialist accordingly finds his basis, as
well as his facts, outside of his mind ; and instead of
inquiring into the intellectual element in his experience, he denies that it has any.   Like all other things,
his experience is not mental but material.

With the facts the laws are also given, being the
threads on which the facts are strung, like beads.   The
thread does not exist for the beads, but the beads for
the thread ; if by some legerdemain we can get the
thread, we are willing to drop the beads.   Modern
science has discovered the art of getting laws which
are independent of facts.   It is still more easy, and
also more popular just now, naïvely to take facts
themselves for laws of limitless application.   Peace of
mind and simplicity are promoted by searching for
nothing beyond the facts and the laws binding them
together.   To look for anything behind what is

directly given by the senses savors too much of the
savage running behind the mirror to discover the person looking at him. Materialists know that there is
nothing behind, and they are perfectly familiar with
what things are in themselves, since they constantly
see, handle, weigh, and measure them—never dealing
with things as they seem to the mind, but only as they
are *per se*, materialism is so solid and its conclusions
are so final. It is the absolute philosophy, just because there is absolutely nothing under the surface on
which it builds.

Corollary.—The purity of materialism will depend
mainly on mental simplicity and intellectual innocence.

Second First Principle. Sensation.

" There is nothing in our understanding which did not enter
through the door of the senses."—MOLESCHOTT.

The old saying that there is nothing in the intellect
which had not first been in the sense has been perverted by adding : " *except the intellect.*" The psychology of materialism begins with the senses and ends
there ; everything else in the mind must therefore be
reduced to this level. A purely intellectual element
would be as destructive of materialism as the sun is
fatal to darkness. For its firm basis on sensation our
philosophy is indebted to Locke rightly interpreted.
Unfortunately, this philosopher was not consistent ;
for after making the mind a blank sheet of a paper on
which matter can scribble laws, he strangely enough
introduced " reflection" as an independent element,
which, as every materialist knows, is a dangerous fac-

tor unless subjected to the control of the senses. Some
of his disciples, however, avoided his error, and
brought science to its present marvellous perfection,
because they just let nature print itself on the blank
sheet. During last century his French followers were
the leading materialists, because they rejected his
error, and carried his sensational principles to their
legitimate conclusions—a performance specially credit-
able, since with their native tact they could have
saved themselves, by proper circumlocution, from all
religious unpleasantness resulting from a bold enuncia-
tion of their views. Their heroic nature and con-
scientiousness, however, scorned all moral and religious considerations, which are still a bugbear among
the uncultivated in America and England.

Modern materialism promises ultimately not to be a
whit behind its French forerunner, and in some respects is already its peer. It is the pure and final product of sensationalism, freed from the vice of reflection, and is affected neither by Berkeley's Idealism,
nor Hume's Scepticism ; neither by Scotch Common
Sense, nor by German Criticism.

Third First Principle.   Scientific Method.

" Baron von Liebig pronounces the materialists dilettanti—
surely a severe epithet to be applied to men who boast so much
of their exactness in natural science, and who for the most part
regard their whims as facts empirically established. But they
can comfort themselves that what Liebig is pleased to call dilet-
tanteism is characteristic of the widest circles engaged in the investigation of nature. Obscurity respecting the history of the
development of their own science ; a confounding of facts, hypotheses, and subjective fancies ; swearing by theoretical dogmas

of the most doubtful character ; passionate impatience in the construction of theories—these are evils which, especially in Germany, are constantly attached, like leaden weights, to natural science, and hinder and paralyze the mighty power of its eagle-flight."—F. A. LANGE, *History of Materialism.*

I have quoted the above for the sake of the facts, not to indorse the censure. The modern method, as all its devotees know, is the grandest achievement of the sublimest intellectual evolution in history. It is not a disgrace, but its glory, that it is opposed by bigots, old fogies, and obscurantists.

The final science is the paradise of hypotheses, and it proudly looks on these as good for food, and " to be desired to make one wise." Like a deluge, modern genius has poured its brilliant scintillations and ingenious theories into science, which has consequently made such progress that Bacon and Newton, not to say anything of Aristotle, would not recognize it. Scientific invention has become so popular that every man with a vivid imagination is inspired to add his quota to the originality of nature.

There is but one reliable method in scientific research—namely, to adopt an hypothesis, and then to search for the facts required for proof and illustration. Those facts which contradict it are, of course, foreign to the hypothesis, and therefore must be laid aside where they belong. Frequently, however, even such facts can, with a little ingenuity, be suitably explained ; and it is one of the richest endowments of a scientist, and one of his chief functions, to select, explain, and adapt his facts wisely. Facts are, however, of secondary importance, the adoption of hypotheses being the main thing. Those who have not enough

buoyancy of fancy to invent their own hypotheses
adopt those of more original minds.   When a favorite
teacher has advanced an important theory, humble
and devout pupils prove their devotion to science by
abusing all who test it and find it wanting.   The master cannot always invent both the hypothesis and proof ;
hence the latter must often be left to the faithful
disciple.   To avoid awkward predicaments, the pupil
should observe carefully when the teacher changes his
views, otherwise he might advocate dogmas which are
no longer orthodox.   A weathercock should always
indicate which way the wind blows ; that is his sole
mission.

Before the invention of steamboats, railroads, tele-
graphs, and electric lights, scientists also proposed hypotheses to account for phenomena ; but they placed
so little confidence in them that they did not regard
them as established until they had viewed them in every
light, had studied all their bearings, and had examined
the facts to see whether they were really explained
thereby and were confirmatory of the hypotheses.   I
speak of the pedants who strictly followed that antiquated method invented centuries ago by a Mr. Bacon,
who made no experiments himself, and consequently
had no idea what labors and difficulties his method
would entail on posterity.   He and his followers held
the strange doctrine that whatever cannot stand the
severest test of facts and of the most searching investigation is not true !   We have cast this and similar
superstitions into the oblivion of the past.   Their cow-
ardly hesitation and bigoted scepticism naturally im-
peded the progress of science.   After the discovery of
America, was not its existence established, however

much men might demonstrate that it could not exist ? The same holds true in science : the discovery of an hypothesis establishes it, all facts and arguments to the contrary notwithstanding.

The inductive method, still followed by a few obscure men, is not adapted to our progressive age. But the deductive is fashionable, and will soon be universal. It is creative and inspirational, instinctively scents the secrets of nature, trips lightly over difficulties, sees no Alps, makes its progress by leaps, has immense assurance and limitless capacities. Its followers, " after having violently and confusedly rummaged among the details of a group, plunge with a sudden spring into the mother-notion. They see it then in its entirety ; they perceive the powers which organize it ; they reproduce it by divination ; they depict in miniature, by the most expressive words, the strangest ideas ; they are not capable of decomposing it into regular series ; they always perceive in a lump. . . . They have a vision of distant effects or living actions ; they are revealers or poets."*

In order to promote finality in science, things once settled materially should not be subjected to unsettlement by new investigations. A different method would involve everything in uncertainty. When an inventor has discovered a theory which includes necessary laws, let it be fearlessly adopted as a guide for the discovery and explanation of facts.

Scientific literature is reaping such rich harvests from the deductive method, that it would be a work of supererogation to pick out examples for illustration.

---

* Taine, " History of English Literature."

Continental scholars accord to England the honor of having given a mighty impulse to the new scientific or deductive method, and that, too, without the slightest evidence of jealousy! Largely to that land belongs the glory of making the barren steppes of science luxuriant with philosophical speculations within the last thirty years. In the hurricane of scientific progress a new spirit has taken possession of men—a spirit which helps us to understand the power of materialism. Professor Virchow, speaking of the transition from the inductive to the deductive method, says : " There came a time when men said, What is the use of observation? if one thinks correctly, it must be possible to construct all things ; everything must be self-evident. A time came when nature was represented as it may be conceived according to a superficial view of things. Our own youth belonged to that period." Though he condemns this spirit, he has evidently read aright the signs of the times. He says in the same address : * " Now, I must say, that there probably seldom was a time in which great problems were treated so frivolously ; yes, not only so frivolously, but even so foolishly. If the only problem presented were this—to take a certain number of the phenomena which present themselves to the mind, and to draw from them a plausible theory, then we could all take our seat in the great arm-chair, and might, as is customary in our day, light a cigar and, while smoking it, finish the theory."

The deductive method is more essential to materialism than matter itself ; for without this method mat-

---

* Proceedings of the German Anthropological Society, 1882.

ter could never meet all the requirements of the case ; but even if there were no matter, this method could easily supply the stuff.

Fourth First Principle. Metaphysics.

"Speculation is philosophy intoxicated."—FEUERBACH.

"To banish from physical Science properly so called, and to relegate to Metaphysics all knowledge which cannot be reduced to numerical expression, is a dangerous abuse of language."—DUKE OF ARGYLL.

When science was still an infant it received maternal aid from metaphysics ; but having now attained maturity it needs no parental help. Comte declared that the theological era belongs to the past, that metaphysics is in its death-struggle, and that the scientific or Positive day is dawning ; and a statement made by so eminent an authority cannot be questioned. Whether metaphysics is identified with psychology, as is done by some final scientists, or whether it is viewed as logic, or whether it is held to be a discussion of the principles of knowledge, or whatever it may be, every materialist feels that it is too wild and vague to deserve even a definition. Lange, in his "History of Materialism," declares that a lack of philosophical culture is, with few exceptions, a characteristic of the German scientist of the day, and many other writers confirm this statement. There is no reason for limiting the remark to German scientists. Every man who inherits his science can dispense with philosophical studies, and will move along more confidently by ignoring the problems which they suggest.

It would, however, be a serious mistake to suppose that scientists are not metaphysical. There is a class of philosophers who, in the progress of thought, regard a lower development related to the higher as the flower is related to the fruit : the flower is not destroyed, but is developed and taken up and conserved in the fruit. So final science does not destroy metaphysics, but conserves the same by affectionately taking it into its bosom. Materialists are abundantly able to do their own speculating, and their works prove that they have all the freedom and variety which in former ages characterized the wildest vagaries of metaphysics. Being outdone in their own specialty by materialists, metaphysicians have fallen into merited contempt. If we can retain physics, we can afford to cast metaphysics to the dogs, where we sent logic some time ago. Vogt and Büchner, not to mention a host of others in and out of Germany, are at least innocent of the metaphysics of the school, and their works cannot merely dispense with logic, but their conclusions gain force without it ; while Mr. Herbert Spencer gives numerous striking illustrations of the fact that, in its methods and dreams, science may develop (perhaps unconsciously) the flowers of metaphysics into the fruits of the Synthetic Philosophy, while at the same time it metaphysically abuses metaphysics.

Fifth First Principle. Absolute Knowledge.

" Science is knowledge certain and evident in itself, or by the principles from which it is deduced or with which it is certainly connected."—FLEMING.

Science consists of facts and laws, reduced to system and established beyond question. Since it cannot err, all errors in its name simply assume its spotless garb in order to gain currency. Whatever has a modern scientific flavor is as reliable as it is true.

The infallibility of science is also an attribute of those material scientists who have absorbed the principles and conclusions of their teachers. Disputes rarely arise among them ; and if they occur, the truth is settled by an appeal to the original authority in such matters, or by a vote of the majority. The absoluteness of these scientists, of course, makes contradictions extremely rare, and those which are found in their works are no doubt in the things themselves, and are essential elements of knowledge. Old Protagoras taught that contradictory assertions are equally true, and Hegel enunciated the doctrine that contradiction is an essential element of thought—a very comforting doctrine in those departments where hardly two agree in their opinions !

Final scientists take the place formerly occupied by theologians. Modern science is Queen in the realm of knowledge, and she makes her devotees the ministers and almoners of truth. Owing to her distinguished favors, those whom she endows can dispense with pursuits necessary to ordinary scholars. What the high-priests of her mysteries do not understand is not worth knowing. They know just what could occur in history and what was impossible ; and since science is prevision, an equation will yet be found for determining what must come to pass in the future. They are masters of morals, religion, and statesmanship, without wasting time in their study. Indeed, brooding over such things might unfit them for materialism. They have discovered that the study of the

classics has an antiquating tendency, and, in their
opinion, their absolute science should be substituted
for them in the schools.   A great point in education
would be gained if the old humanities were banished
and if our culture could be based on a study of the
humanities found in brutes.   Formerly man was
studied in human, but now in natural, history.

The developments made by modern science enable
men to take to it as naturally as fish to water ; and
they become eminent in it without that severe mental
discipline which was requisite in former ages.   Boys
catch the scientific spirit from the master ; and the
scientific lad who cannot echo his teacher's sneer at
the faith of Newton, Pascal, Faraday, and Maxwell is
not very bright.

It is the absolute knowledge of our popular scientists which has overturned the superstition of the day.
They have popularized science, and have made the
people masters of its spirit.   They are found everywhere, and may, perhaps, some day deliver Royal
Academy lectures.   Instead of confining themselves to
the severer methods of the dark ages, and spending
their time in laboratories, they prefer to hold the public by the ear, whenever it is long enough.

Sixth First Principle.   Necessary Truth.

" How far what we now regard as ' necessary truths ' may require modification in the future, it is impossible for us to judge,
simply because we can no more conceive of anything beyond the
range of mental development we have ourselves attained than a
man born blind can picture visual objects."—W. B. CARPENTER.

Whatever may be required by the hypothesis
adopted by materialists is called an axiom.   Being a

necessity to the hypothesis, it is, of course, a necessary truth. These truths, on account of their mathematical certainty, are of great consequence. After an axiom has been deduced from an hypothesis it requires no further investigation, but is ready for immediate use.

Thus, if the opinion is adopted that matter accounts for everything, then it is a necessary truth that there is nothing but matter in the universe. We may not know what matter is, nor how it works, nor is this essential ; but we do know with absolute certainty that there cannot possibly be anything but matter. To this axiom materialism is tethered. So when the view is held that there is no design in nature, it becomes a necessary truth that all design must be explained as not design, but as the result of natural selection or something else. If we make man a descendant of the ape, it is a necessary truth that all his faculties are the same as those of monkeys, only developed. After an opinion has been adopted it is easy to get the necessary truth required for proof. The effort to demonstrate the peculiar axioms of final science would be Quixotic.

Seventh First Principle. Matter.

" In matter all the natural and mental forces reside ; in it alone can they be revealed. Matter is the primitive source of all existence."—Büchner.

" Against the calm but effective weapons of physical and physiological materialism, the enemies of the same cannot stand ; the conflict is too unequal. It contends with facts which each one can see and seize ; but its enemies, with surmises and hypotheses."—Büchner.

This principle has nothing to do with the definition of matter ; its aim is to establish the fact that matter

exists, and that besides it there is nothing else.   After
this has been settled the definition can be considered
if thought advisable.   We know infinitely more
about matter before we try to define it than afterward.
This knowledge is here utilized.

Every materialist knows that it is absurd to demonstrate the existence of matter, since it is of all things
the most palpable.   It reveals itself directly to every
sense, and the denial of its existence is the denial of
all thought.   Equally absurd is it to believe in the
existence of anything immaterial or supersensible.
Whoever does this is superstitious, is afraid of ghosts,
and utterly lacks the scientific spirit.   If we admit
anything but matter, what would become of materialism ?

It might be an herculean undertaking to prove that
there are only material forces, since it implies a perfect knowledge of those forces ; but where there's a
will there's a way.   Büchner's word may be taken
for the demonstration : " The scientist proves—and
that with satisfactory evidence—that there are no
other than physical, chemical, and mechanical forces
in nature, and then he draws the incontrovertible conclusion that by them the organisms, too, must have
been generated and developed.   How this formation
has in every case proceeded or is proceeding is comprehended by the science of the day only in a small
degree, and will, perhaps, never be fully comprehended ; but it does not doubt that it is so."   This
last point is the essential thing : " it does not doubt."
I have not been able to discover his proof " with satisfactory evidence ;" but that's a small matter.   How
unscientific it would be first to prove that organisms

and all other existences *are* the product of material forces, and then to infer that no others exist! After fully persuading ourselves that there are only " physical, chemical, and mechanical forces," is it not an incontrovertible conclusion that organisms, spirit, and whatever else exists is the product of these forces? This is one of the necessary truths of materialism. *How* it is no one knows ; *that* it is the materialist " does not doubt." The mysteries of life and consciousness are absolutely impenetrable ; therefore, we know that they are purely material products.

Corollary.—This principle makes it evident why a final scientist is a final authority. There is nothing but matter ; the materialist understands matter perfectly ; therefore, he knows everything.

Eighth First Principle.   Probabilism.

" They assented to things that were neither evident nor certain but only probable."—SOUTH.

Probabilism plays so conspicuous a part in modern science that we are justified in making it one of the most important principles. Much that cannot be demonstrated can be made to seem probable, and then may be used to promote scientific accuracy and certainty. There is an entire school of scientists who have become notorious by converting theories into dogmas, mere facts into laws, and probabilities into certainties.

One advantage of this first principle is that it gives so much latitude to its manipulator. Our preferences, inclinations, needs, and whims may help probabilities

and improbabilities along much more than facts and
arguments.   Hence the beautiful variety in the probabilities of modern philosophers.   Of two equally probable suppositions, the philosopher takes the one which
suits his theories the best ; he can then regard it as
demonstrated or as a necessary truth, and may denounce every other view as unscientific.   Probabilism
gives that freedom of which religious bigots want to
rob science.

Illustrations of the use of this principle could be
given *ad nauseam* from the final natural philosophy ;
and for its popularity the world is largely indebted to
Mr. Darwin and Mr. Herbert Spencer.   Those familiar with their works soon learn that a thing may at
one time be very probable, then very doubtful, and at
last certain.   Scientific opinions are like stock, whose
value depends on the state of the market.   What a
genius cautiously proposes as probable or at least possible, a faithful disciple can use as certain.   It is so
much more agreeable to inherit an estate with a clear
title than one that is in litigation.

A volume which lately appeared in the interest of
Darwinism, and which Mr. Darwin was desirous of
having " broadcast," declares that probability is " the
guide of science" as well as of " common life."   " The
business of science, as of common life, is to estimate
correctly the relative degrees of probability presented
by this or that theory or hypothesis."   Yes, and there
are some departments in which this seems to be the
whole of science.   Speaking of evolution, this author
says : " But when a theory has been raised to such a
level of probability as this, it is, for all practical purposes, as good as a demonstration."   Certainly, we

may make it so probable in order that we can use it ; and when once "as good as a demonstration," it needs no more investigation. He, in fact, claims that nothing more is needed "to add to the strength of our belief in, as distinguished from our knowledge of, the truth of evolution." Some have a scientific "belief" which is so strong that it cannot be affected by any demonstration. Faith is the substance of things hoped for and the evidence of things not seen, but needed to prop up a favorite theory. Can any one still doubt that modern science has taken the place of religion ?

In the same volume we find that this principle is a corner-stone of modern science. "The doctrine of natural selection, therefore, depends for its validity on the doctrine of organic evolution ; for if once the doctrine of organic evolution were established, no one would dispute that much of the adaptation was probably effected by natural selection. *How* much we cannot say—probably never shall be able to say ; for even Mr. Darwin himself does not doubt that other causes besides that of natural selection have assisted in the modifying of specific types. For the sake of simplicity, however, I shall not go into the subject, but shall always speak of natural selection as the only cause of organic evolution." Splendid ! *If* organic evolution were established, no one would dispute that *much* of the adaptation was *probably* effected by natural selection, though *how* much no one knows. For simplicity's sake, I "shall *always* speak of natural selection as the *only* cause of organic evolution."

This principle is providentially provided for materialism, which uses it with a lavish generosity. And it may be of great service in harmonizing science and

religion. Probabilism has played a conspicuous part
in religion, especially in Jesuistic morality. After
having thus been religiously approved, there is no
wonder that it has become so popular with certain
natural philosophers.

Ninth First Principle. Humility.

" Levelling all within reach of his hand, even the loftiest things
—especially the loftiest."—TAINE.

We materialists are extremely humble, cheerfully
admitting our ignorance of all we can neither demonstrate, nor include in an hypothesis, nor use as a
necessary truth, nor find probable because useful.
But in another sense lowliness of mind is a characteristic of materialism ; it always goes to the bottom of
things and stays there. Of two principles which
equally well account for phenomena it always finds
it probable that the lowest is the correct one, and consequently makes that the rule for interpreting what is
highest. By thus getting at the base of things, it
makes everything conform philosophically to the
basest. By bringing the sublime on a level with the
lowest, we exalt the lowest to the height of the sublime. From the dirt which sticks to a root a materialist can tell what fruit the tree must bear ; his insight, therefore, enables him to dispense with the tree
and fruit if he has the dirt. He can take any excres-
cence of religion, and by reducing all spirituality to it
he can materially account for all religion, and if so
disposed can explain it away. The same is true of
morality. According to this principle, it requires no

extraordinary genius to make man a developed brute. The dignity of man is no obstacle after he has been deprived of it, and very naturally materialists are indignant when asked to take that into account after they have made it of no account. We, the heirs of the ages, cannot be expected to hold the antiquated notion of the heathen Greeks, that man is the measure of all things, for that leads to anthropomorphism ; therefore the animal is the measure of man. Matter can evolve spirit ; but of course spirit cannot produce matter ; therefore there is matter, but no spirit. There may be mind as the result of evolution, but there could be none at its beginning. If there are evidences of reason in nature, then it is the product of matter or it is not reason. Scientific wonders can be performed by getting things to the bottom and keeping them there !

Tenth First Principle. The Materialistic Mood.

"Hail, divinest Melancholy !"—MILTON.

Philosophic thinkers who read materialistic works without the necessary training for their doctrines may wonder how the author can believe his own arguments, or can expect them to convince others. The fault, however, is not with the author, but with the readers. Were they in his mood, they too would feel that materialism is the maëlstrom which swallows all that comes within reach. Its great power lies in certain dispositions, inclinations, and views of life, which give their coloring to the philosophic and scientific pursuits and tendencies. The novice in materialism imagines

that arguments are the bulwarks of his system ; but
he who has long felt its power, and has fathomed its
depths and shallows, and has, so to speak, passed
through it, knows that it is, above all, a thing of
moods, on whose proper culture its progress depends.
With these moods its arguments, sometimes furnished
by them, are omnipotent ; without them they are im-
potent.

There are states in which a man cannot be a materialist ; there are others so serene, so blissful, that he
becomes one naturally, without facts, without reason.
There are natural hyloists as well as idealists. But
these moods are also subject to discipline. One may,
by means of his studies and training, become so thoroughly intellectual in his tastes as to be wholly unable
to appreciate our arguments. The mind may have
been so perverted by education as still to continue its
inquiries after matter has been found as the ultimate
thing ; it may persist in seeking something behind the
atoms—something working in and through them ; and
by this obstinacy it may penetrate through matter to
mind, and claim for the latter the priority and superiority ! By so studying the spirit as to become intensely conscious of it, a man may at last be unable
to deny it, or may lose sight of its purely material
character ; by cherishing certain ideals he may be so
far exalted above matter that he becomes unable to
lose himself in it ; the reason may be so trained as
presumptuously to go behind the harmless, unsus-
pecting assumptions of materialism, absurdly to ask
for reasons where there are none, and for the explanation of things which are taken for granted as final ;
and the logic of a man may be so lame that it is incapa-

ble of the grand leaps which land in our conclusions.

There are others who are natural materialists—earth's noblest sons. They love matter as both their father and mother, and as dutiful children they defend and protect it ; cheerfully and without difficulty they limit their thoughts to it, and make it their scientific guide. Their mental system is a pyramid : broad base, all matter, its size diminishing with its height, not quite reaching the stars. Under it the solid earth, over it the air, fit only for air-castles. A grand structure, and valuable because a tomb.

The emotions must be carefully disciplined if the materialistic mood is to be attained. It may be safest to suppress them altogether. Science is a Stoic. The notion of some philosophers that it should be in harmony with the whole man, ignoring none of his claims, conflicting with none of his real interests, considering all his faculties, powers, tendencies, is nonsense. It does not take into account the mind and heart and conscience, but these must adapt themselves to science, which is complete if in unison with matter. Materialism seeks the truth, the whole truth, and nothing but the truth ; therefore it has nothing to do with hope or fear, with the dignity of man or the interests of the spirit. Materialistic perfection is attained when its pyramid tomb is so complete that hope, and fear, and joy, and remorse, and spirit, and God, and immortality find room in the eternal darkness of its cavern.

Materialism and Pessimism are twins and co-laborers. What the one sows the other reaps, and the harvest is shared between them. Buoyancy of spirit may lift

the soul so high that its affectional tendencies will lead
it to seek its affinities beyond matter. But gloom,
deep and universal, promotes materialism. The dark
mood is most scientific. If the materialist cannot be
found in the mind, look for him in the liver.

Last First Principle.   Corrective System.

" I now admit, after reading the essay by Nägeli on plants, and
the remarks by various authors with respect to animals, more
especially those recently made by Professor Broca, that in the
earlier editions of my ' Origin of Species ' I probably attributed
too much to the action of natural selection, or the survival of the
fittest. I have altered the fifth edition of the Origin so as to
confine my remarks to adoptive changes of structure. I had not
formerly sufficiently considered the existence of many structures
which appear to be, as far as we can judge, neither beneficial nor
injurious ; and this I believe to be one of the greatest oversights
as yet detected in my work."—DARWIN.

The Corrective System is the keystone in the arch
of materialistic principles. Whatever materialists accept as true is final ; for according to the principles
already given, they advocate only mathematical definiteness and certainty. But it frequently happens,
after a matter has been finally settled, that supple-
mentary evidence overturns all that had been firmly
and eternally established. These unexpected developments would be very embarrassing if science had no
corrective system ; but with it in vigorous operation
there can be no confusion. For instance, a materialist
infers *à priori* through his senses what the properties
of matter are, and then uses them in explaining the
universe. Then something is discovered which they
cannot explain. By an application of the corrective

system matter is then so amended as to account for the
new phenomenon. It may also happen that in his im-
pulsive generosity he has endowed matter with properties now no longer necessary ; then they are simply
eliminated. No one thinks of objecting to this new
endowment, or the elimination of an old one, since it
is needed in order to keep matter in trim to explain
all things, as it is known to do. We consequently
endow matter with working and latent properties,
similar to active and latent heat. When materialists
discover a property, it is in the working state ; if
afterward it is not found, then it has retired to the
latent state ; and if a new property is needed, we
simply advance it from the latent to the active state.
This can be done *ad infinitum* without the least protest from matter—a striking evidence of the correctness of the method and a singular confirmation of materialism ! In its process of development matter is
constantly transforming its latent into active powers.
In its inorganic state some of the properties are latent,
which work as soon as an organism is to be produced.
Since Mr. Spencer has defined life, the inorganic produces organisms much more easily than formerly, for
it now knows that life is " the definite combination
of heterogeneous changes, both simultaneous and suc-
cessive, in correspondence with external co-existences
and sequences." Before this it worked in the dark.
Some properties of matter lie dormant until they are
needed to produce consciousness, reason, conscience,
and spirituality. It may yet be discovered that these
properties are not latent at all, but that they are created by matter when it attains a certain maturity of
evolution. But whatever endowment or elimination

or creation may take place, we know that all the forces
at work in the universe are in matter and have been
there from all eternity, and that nothing else exists.

There are numerous other Principles, but they can
easily be deduced from the foregoing. For fear, however, that it might otherwise be overlooked, I here
emphasize the fact that science and philosophy must be
used as synonyms. An important point will be gained
by conferring on philosophy the absoluteness of
science.

CHAPTER III.

MATTER.

" Of the ultimate nature of matter the human faculties cannot take cognizance ; nor can data bo furnished by observation or experiment on which to found an investigation of it. All wo know of it is its sensible properties."—BRANDE.

" Matter and force, so far as wo know, are mere names for certain forms of consciousness."—HUXLEY.

WHOEVER consistently follows the Principles of the preceding chapter will hardly discover anything supersensible in the universe. Indeed, it has already been made one of our first principles that nothing but matter can exist ; it is, therefore, demonstrated. This necessary truth is no new invention ; some of the ancient sages also regarded it as an axiom. Thus Democritus taught that "the principles of all things are the atoms and empty space ; everything else is mere opinion." Such opinions must consequently be rigorously banished from science.

Having now a firm hold on matter we can explain it, and thus get at the heart of the universe. At first we are amazed to find that no satisfactory definition of matter is current ; but on reflection we learn that all the most evident things are most difficult to define. Some things lose sensibly by defining them rationally. We comprehend matter so perfectly without a definition that it may be wisest not to hamper our-

selves with explanations of its nature. Much medita-
tion on the subject is unhealthy. It cannot be denied
that every profound thinker who undertakes to get a
clear and exhaustive conception of matter runs the risk
of finding at last a mere name instead of the thing
itself—an abstract term and an empty shell—and thus
the only real and tangible substance loses itself in an
abstraction. I should here, after very mature deliberation, follow the usual method of taking matter as it
is, and using it to the best advantage, without the risk
of a definition, if I were writing only for materialists;
but for the sake of the unscientific a definition must be
attempted.

Those who are thoroughly initiated into the secrets
of nature know just what is required in defining matter. The fact that it is the only reality is the most
essential guide in our efforts to define it. Being the
beginning, the substance, the end of all existence, the
definition meeting this requirement is correct. Somehow the dictionaries (Littré, with the French materialists before him not excepted), cyclopædias, and scientific works do not meet the case; they leave the impression that what everybody can seize no mind knows.
After laboriously examining all definitions of ancient
and modern times, I find that this is the sum total:
matter is matter. This definition is perfect, except
that it lacks definiteness; I shall therefore give my
own. *Matter is all that is.* This is at the same time
definite without giving any obstinate or objectionable
marks to interfere with progress. Etymology, which
always indicates what things were originally, not what
people thought of them, confirms the above view.
Matter is from mater, which means mother. This

demonstrates that matter was originally the mother of animals, men, and gods, as well as of the rest of the universe ; it is therefore the creator of all that is.

I had already written that my concise and yet comprehensive definition was final, when I lighted upon a sharp and lucid one by. Professor Tyndall, which rivals mine, and also meets all requirements. In speaking of the nine months of gestation, and of the wonders of the human body formed and developed in that period, he says : " All this has been accomplished, not only without man's contrivance, but without his knowledge, the secret of his own organization having been withheld from him since his birth in the immeasurable past until the other day. Matter I define as that mysterious thing by which all this is accomplished. How it came to have this power is a question on which I never ventured an opinion." * I always come back to this definition with increasing admiration, and am willing to adopt it as final. It harmonizes perfectly with my own and with science, and has some advantages which it would be difficult to put into any other language. " *Matter I define as that mysterious thing by which all this is accomplished.*" Matter is here shown to be a " thing ;" this thing is " mysterious ;" and the whole work of gestation is accomplished by this mysterious thing labelled " Matter." Those who have not been trained scientifically may be tempted to interpose all kinds of impertinent questions, as these : " Is the declaration that matter is mysterious an explanation of it ? If it is mysterious, how do we know *what* it is ? How do we know that

---

* *Fortnightly Review*, 1875, p. 598.

it is matter ?   How do we know that it, without any
other power, accomplished the entire work of developing the wonderful form of man ?"   Such questions
are utterly unscientific, and in this respect are in striking contrast with the definition.   The uninitiated of
course cannot comprehend the wonderful beauty and
adaptability of this explanation of matter.   Since it is
a mystery, we can endow it as we please and as emergencies require, and then defy the world to prove that
it has not these endowments.   If after all our explanation of things something remains unexplained, we
simply refer it to this mystery, which does not become
a whit more mysterious by heaping on it other mysteries.   By thus getting hold of the soul of all being,
and by handling it, turning it over, and contemplating
it on all sides, we are prepared to meet the shallow
pretext that the known properties of matter cannot
explain mental and spiritual phenomena.   These phenomena are explained by the mysterious, not the
known, properties of matter.

Having thus found a mystery which is so perfectly
understood that we see in it the primary cause of all
that transpires, we can dispense with God as well as
with reason.   He must be a simpleton who does not
comprehend that there absolutely cannot be anything
but that matter which is the mystery which interprets
everything.   If anything else existed it would only
be so much stuff lying around loose.

Proudly conscious of the inestimable service thereby
rendered exact science, I joyfully spread Mr. Tyndall's scientific demonstration of the nature of matter.
By means of this demonstration science has attained
self-consciousness, and matter so fully understands its

properties that it readily distinguishes itself from all foreign admixture. When this definition has penetrated philosophic minds and illuminated the scientific atmosphere, all the silly twaddle of sceptics about the impossibility of defining matter will cease. After the egg has been made to stand on end, will there be any more fools to question whether it can be done ?

With singular unanimity the scientists and philosophers, the modern popular ones alone excepted, affirm that matter is a mystery ; but they do not all see that consequently, by mathematical calculation, there is nothing in the universe besides. According to Mill (Logic, I. 68), " Our conception of a body is that of an unknown cause of sensations ;" that body " is the mysterious something which excites the mind to feel." He declares that " it is necessary to remark that on the inmost nature of the thinking principle, as well as on the inmost nature of matter, we are, and with our faculties must always remain, in the dark." Materialists are not often stirred with gratitude to stern logicians, but we are devoutly thankful to Mr. Mill for his unintentional help. Since two things equal to the same thing are equal to each other, it is evident that from the above materialism can be established. Thrown into the form of a syllogism, the argument stands thus : Matter is a mystery ; Mind is a mystery; therefore, mind is matter, or, which is the same thing, matter is mind.

After thus settling what matter is, we have no difficulty in determining what it can do. It can do just anything and everything required of it. The process, like all other mysteries when once explained, is so simple that those who understand it cannot compre-

hend how others can see any difficulty. The scientific
materialistic method is this : it first settles the point
that something called matter exists ; then it takes for
granted, as a necessary truth, that there neither is nor
can be anything but matter ; this axiom proves that
all existence must somehow be the product of matter ;
after that has been successfully accomplished, this
method examines the material things, and from them
learns what matter is.

The reasoning thus forms a perfect circle, and those
whose minds are properly constructed to accept it as
final are not likely to be affected by any arguments
against their position. Materialism lies on the outside
of things where the senses discover it and pick it up ;
this makes it so self-evident that it is strongest without reason—that fruitful source of error and per-
plexity !

Coming to think of the matter, matter itself is of no
earthly use whatever ; but it is essential as a receptacle
for the forces which work in nature. Aside from
these it is so helpless that it cannot even communicate
with the senses. When the mind reflects on matter
(that is, on itself, as demonstrated above), it cannot
find anything to which imagination can cling after the
forces are gone. Carpenter (" Mental Physiology")
says : " It is now generally admitted that we neither
know nor can know anything of *Matter*, save through
the medium of the impressions it makes on our senses ;
and those impressions are only derived from the
Forces of which Matter is the vehicle ;" and he adds
that " there seems valid ground for the assertion that
our notion of *Matter* is a conception of the Intellect,
Force being that externality of which we have the

most direct—perhaps even the *only* direct—cognizance." As Brande says of matter : " All we know of it is its sensible properties ;" and to these materialism clings tenaciously, and thrusting its hand through the forces, it grasps solid matter itself.

Since matter exists only for the sake of force, we could dispense with it altogether if something else could be found to hold the forces, or if we could get them to hold themselves ; but as this is scarcely possible—at least, not for materialism—we shall stick to matter, with the distinct understanding, however, that it must adjust itself to the forces for whose sake it exists. It is an axiom that it must receive all the forces in the universe ; this was well considered in giving our definition of matter, in which everything distinctive receives so wide a berth that there is abundant room for all that is real and imaginary.

The definition of force given by Mayer is good enough for practical purposes—" Something which is expended in producing motion." Of the nature of force we know nothing, and in this respect it is equal to matter. Our ignorance of what force is in itself is of incalculable value to the modern scientist, since it enables him to exercise the greater ingenuity in determining its nature. Thus he knows with absolute certainty that all the forces reside in matter ; that they have been there from eternity ; that they cannot exist independently of matter ; that these natural forces produce everything that exists ; and that, *nolens volens*, all that is must be reduced to these forces, or rather to force, for there is but one, just as there is but one matter. Now, since force produces motion only, it is evident that motion must be made to ac-

count for everything. After its postulates are properly
fixed, materialism finds it a necessary truth that everything mental and material is a result of motion.
"Thought is a movement of matter," Moleschott
says; and let him who has the temerity to question
the statement prove the contrary. No one has ever
seen motion produce thought, nor has any evidence
been given that it does, nor can any one imagine how
this is possible. But this is not to the point. It may
be imagined *that* motion does it, which is sufficient to
establish the fact.

There are thinkers who claim that we get our idea
of force from the will ; and the inference has thus been
drawn that our knowledge of force comes from our
minds rather than from external objects. Such metaphysical reflections run the risk of making the forces
mental rather than material. Materialism is safer in
stoutly insisting that it has nothing to do with the *idea*
of force, but that it deals directly with force as found
by the senses in matter. Its force is not rational, but
sensible ; it is not a product of thought, but thought
is the product of force.

After materialists had long ago settled that matter
can accomplish everything, they had the mortification
of meeting objections from persons respecting whom
they cherished the brightest hopes. Mr. Huxley's
words, put at the head of this chapter to inspire materialists with new enthusiasm, are dangerous : " Matter and force, so far as we know, are mere names for
certain forms of consciousness." That is an inversion
which is a perversion, as already shown. They are
not forms of consciousness, but consciousness is certain
forms of matter and force. With deep regret we also

read these words from him : "When Materialists
stray beyond the borders of their path and begin to
talk of there being nothing but matter and force and
necessary laws, I decline to follow them." How can
a man be a materialist if he admits that there is anything else? "Stray beyond the borders of their
path"? How is that possible when that path has no
borders?

It has repeatedly been demonstrated theoretically
by materialists that organisms are the product of inorganic matter ; indeed, spontaneous generation is a
fundamental article of our creed. If we could only
get the dead stuff properly arranged and environed we
have no doubt that from it living beings would swarm.
Since everything depends on this supposition, we must
insist that it is possible ; and we shall so insist. Now
comes Professor Virchow, and says : "Every man
who attempts to produce an animal or a plant by
means of spontaneous generation fails. This Haeckel
himself admits. Even he now concedes that it is very
doubtful whether in our day we can still calculate on
spontaneous generation ; perhaps it only occurred at a
certain time in the past." Why not? Push it back
as far as possible, only be sure that it was done. That
past spontaneous generation, which saves materialism,
is treated by the Berlin professor as unscientific.
"This, indeed, makes the matter very difficult ; for
if the idea is rejected that at present there is still
spontaneous generation, then the whole subject is with-
drawn from the sphere of empirical investigation ;
then it becomes simply a play of the fancy ; then
there is no possibility of approaching the problem by
means of practical research. For this would only be

possible if we succeeded in making out of inorganic matter a living creature, however small it might be." It is simply monstrous to ask us to prove practically all we believe scientifically. We only claim to prove spontaneous generation theoretically ; we are therefore not affected by Professor Virchow's argument.

It is thus settled that though inorganic matter cannot now be made to produce life, it must have done so in the past ; for the life is here, and there is nothing else but matter from which it could have sprung. But it cannot be denied that men were much more intimate with matter a few years ago than at present. Lately, Professor Du Bois-Reymond upset some final conclusions of materialists in his "Seven Riddles of the World." In a former address he had already clipped the wings of some poetic scientists who knew more about matter than was lawful, but he had mercifully left considerable play to the atoms. But his "riddles" proved a stunner. His final conclusion is, that we do not know the nature or essence of matter and force ; cannot understand the origin of motion or of life ; are unable to explain the evidences of design in nature (and that after Darwin's and Haeckel's works!) ; and that we cannot account for the origin of sensation, of consciousness, of language, of rational thought, and of will ! But if we cannot make matter account for these things now, we insist that it has done so in the past, and will do so in the future ; and we would rather give matter some new endowments than admit its impotence.

CHAPTER IV.

" But a span of that time which stretches both backward and forward into eternity is meted out to man here on earth, and the space which his foot can tread is narrowly bounded above and below ; so also his scientific knowledge finds natural limits in the direction of the infinitely small as well as of the infinitely great. The question of atoms seems to me to lead beyond these limits, and hence I consider it impractical. An atom in itself can no more become an object of our investigation than a differential."— J. R. MAYER.

MATTER is divisible, and the finest particles into which imagination can divide it are called atoms.* They are invisible, and are in no sense objects of sense ; still, in its analysis of matter, the mind must stop somewhere, and it chooses to rest with these in-

---

* To the spiritual materialist the atoms are of interest, because they account for mental as well as physical phenomena. If they could be used for the latter only we should not devote this chapter to them. It is not the atomic theories based on chemical investigations and mathematical calculations which are important to us ; we esteem them because the creative power of the mind can utilize the atoms to promote the final science ; in all other respects we consign them to the chemist and mathematician. Of what earthly interest to materialism is, for instance, the recent calculation which makes the diameters of the atoms of metals, water, and the air about the ten millionth of a centimetre ? That these diameters are material is the only essential part of this minute knowledge.

finitesimal particles.   They are ponderable, but we have nothing so light as to balance one of them.   They are extended, but only just so much as not to be able to occupy less space ; and if an atom were in the least degree less extended, it would not be extended.   If, therefore, an atom is cut in two, each half will occupy as much space as the whole.

Atoms are not things with which we experiment, but they are mere notions.   Mr. Huxley pronounces them "imaginative symbols ;" Du Bois-Reymond declares them a fiction.   One philosopher says : " He who constructs the universe from atoms builds a structure with materials which he has seen in a mirror, and which he imagines he can take thence."*   But what if the atoms are fiction ? That fiction we turn into fact, and on that build the solid structure of the universe.

Mr. Tyndall, speaking of mythology and scientific theories, says : " In both cases our materials drawn from the world of the senses are modified by the imagination to suit intellectual needs.   The ' first beginnings ' of Lucretius were not objects of sense, but they were suggested and illustrated by objects of sense. The idea of atoms proved an early want on the part of minds in pursuit of the knowledge of nature.   It has never been relinquished, and in our own day it is growing steadily in power and precision." †

Materialism can always use ideas if they help it to matter ; and this is the reason why " the *idea* of atoms" is of such immense service.   When the idea has furnished the atoms, materialists drop the " idea"

---

* Teichmüller, " Die wirkliche und die scheinbare Welt," 134.
† *Longman's Magazine*, November, 1882.

and retain the atoms. These are to them not a notion, but a reality ; and in speaking of them, materialists prove that they are perfectly familiar with the atoms themselves. In popular books and addresses, as well as in philosophical works, it is advisable always to speak of atoms as if materialism had subjected their properties to mathematical demonstration. They lie at the basis of all matter, and are " the foundation stones of the universe ;" and unless they can be made the germs of all things they are somehow defective, and have not been properly apprehended. Atoms are the seed from which all being is developed.

In the unwritten history of the imagination few chapters are more interesting than that on the progress of the atoms. Their inventor is not known ; but the first record of them was made by Democritus, and some improvements were suggested by Epicurus and Lucretius. They were then permitted to rest for awhile. In our day, as Mr. Tyndall says, the *idea* of atoms " is growing steadily in power and precision ;" and at the present rate of progress the atoms based on this idea may yet be so evolved as to meet all the emergencies of materialism. In the unwritten chapter we are astonished at their marvellous adaptability and at the submissive spirit with which they have yielded to the transformations necessary to manufacture the universe. On the principle of the corrective system they have, as circumstances required, been subject to great changes ; the only thing about them which materialists made invariable is, that they are matter, and that they are the all-sufficient cause of that which was, and is, and shall be.

The atoms have been inert matter, bare and barren

substances ; force was supposed to inhere in them or to
have been somehow communicated to them, though
viewed in both cases as distinct from the matter in
which it was imprisoned.   Just how matter and force
are united in an atom, if they are united, has never
been logically fancied, and is therefore an open
question.   In the process of evolution through which
the mind put the atoms they ceased to be anything
except centres of force—an excellent arrangement if
able to sustain themselves in that state, and to maintain their omnipotence ; but this condition of the
atoms endangers materialism, and therefore is unscientific.   At one time the atoms were originally at rest ;
but then there was insurmountable difficulty in getting
them to move ; therefore they were originally endowed with motion.   Sometimes the atoms were all
alike, and then there were only quantitative relations,
not qualitative differences.   They retained this state
so long as motion was imagined capable of accounting
for the variety found in the universe ; when the imagination became enfeebled, qualitative differences
were introduced into the atoms.   Their present status
is hard to determine, since they are not stationary
enough to admit of careful examination.   We only
know that their condition just now is extremely variable, and there is scarcely a tune to which they do not
dance.   But in spite of the transformations to which
they are subject, their capacity is by no means exhausted.   Every cosmic philosopher can adjust them
as he pleases ; it does not hurt the atoms.

Enough of their history ; we shall now minutely
examine the primitive dust itself.   Since the atoms
are an unknown x, whose value depends on the equa-

tions we make, it is worth some labor to get proper formulas. The slightest variation of the atoms in our minds would have the most astounding effect on the structure of the universe. They must somehow be brought together and put into a working condition—a problem whose difficulties increase with the efforts at solution. The invention of the first impulse resulting in motion would be the discovery of the perpetual motion of the universe. If the atoms are imagined as originally and eternally at rest, how did they begin to move? By resting so long they would naturally beget an inert habit, and it would be difficult to give them a start. Therefore all research demonstrates that they were originally endowed with motion. If this motion was an eternal falling through infinite space in straight and parallel lines, there is no reason for quitting these lines and forming a union with one another; therefore they quit them by chance or accident, or in some other way. Their motion, however, may not have been of that order at all, but of a kind which would somehow bring the atoms into collision, so as to enable them to begin work. It was necessary to get into business, and the persistence in the parallel lines was simply a waste of time; the atoms must therefore have come together, and it is not material how it was brought about, except that it was done by the atoms, without the interference of will and intelligence. Democritus and Epicurus endowed the atoms originally with motion, which must have been of a character to bring them together, since otherwise they might as well have been left at rest. These philosophers are an authority on this subject, and are the more worthy of confidence because they were nearer the beginning of

things than we, and consequently had better oppor-
tunities for observation.   Indeed, in spite of the vast
progress since their day, they knew just as much about
atoms as our modern materialists.   Lucretius thought
that just as there is at times something arbitrary in
the movements of men and animals, so there may have
been something of the same kind in the motion of the
atoms.   In confirmation of this it may be stated that
nothing to the contrary has ever been proved by their
examination under the microscope.   It may, in fact,
be asserted that all the motion thus far conferred on
them has been arbitrary.

Mr. Tyndall, in the article already quoted, says:
" These atoms are so small, and, when grouped to
molecules, are so tightly clasped together, that they are
capable of tremors equal in rapidity to those of light
and radiant heat.   To a mind coming freshly to these
subjects, the numbers with which scientific men here
habitually deal must appear utterly fantastical ; and
yet to minds trained in the logic of science, they express most sober and certain truth.   The constituent
atoms of molecules can vibrate to and fro millions of
millions of times in a second."   That's so ; and a
mind trained in the science of logic, as well as in " the
logic of science," knows that the atoms will not be
hurt if we make them vibrate billions of billions of
times in the millionth part of the least conceivable
fraction of a second.   Such being their capacity for
motion, it must have been possible for them to so ar-
range themselves originally as to come into collision,
and to shove themselves about so as to move the universe into existence.

Having now sufficiently stirred the atoms to set

them in motion, we shall proceed to determine their original character. This was neither moral nor immoral, neither mental nor spiritual, all of which are more modern attributes ; at that time they were simply and purely material. Gassendi held that atoms are all identical as to substance, but different in figure. Others have held, and for just as good reasons, that they differed in quality, but had the same shape. It may also be that they differed both as to shape and quality. I hold that atoms are all alike in quality and shape ; whence could the difference have come ? As there is no reason why they should differ, we are justified in the belief that they were alike from all eternity. Epicurus states distinctly that nothing must be attributed to them but size, figure, and weight, thus excluding differences of quality. They may have differed in shape, so as to fit into each other ; but this must not be interpreted to mean that they were made so, for they were not made at all ; neither must it be regarded as an evidence of design, for we would rather make them exactly the same in shape than to admit design ; nor must it be taken to mean that there was any difference of length, breadth, or thickness, for this is impossible, since each one occupied just as little space as possible in but one direction. When Mr. Tyndall speaks of them as " clasped together," he does not mean that they have hooks or hands, for they have no room for these ; it is one of those poetic attributes in which the atoms delight. Whether they are clasped together, or glued together, or affectionately embrace one another, is all the same. Indeed, to speak of them as at all touching each other is also a poetic expression, since it has been demonstrated mathematically that they never can come in contact. Poetry has largely had a monopoly of the atoms ever since Lucretius put them into hexameter.

We are fortunate in getting the atoms along safely thus far ; but there is still some difficulty in making them operate, even if we give them attractive and repulsive powers. It is a misfortune little short of a calamity that they cannot touch each other. Newton and even some of the modern philosophers have been puzzled by the problem how a body can work where it is not. The force it exerts must have something to convey it to the place where it is to operate. Of course the force must not be imagined as leaving the body, for it is the very essence of that body, and the one cannot exist without the other. What, then, carries the force where it is to act ? Empty space does not, for in that the force would lose itself, and it might wander about eternally without conveying its message to the right spot. Accordingly, something called ether has been commissioned to carry the forces to their destination.

The modern ether is not the same as that of the ancients. They used it for various purposes, such as the construction of the universe, in breathing a soul into it after it was constructed, and in accounting for the origin of life. They also employed it in forming a heaven for their gods. Since we have no gods, we use it as a heaven for the atoms. According to Hesiod, ether is the product of Erebus and Night ; others made it the offspring of Chaos and Caligo. We avoid all these assumptions by making our ether eternal. We need it only for the explanation of action at a distance, gravitation, light, heat, and electricity.

" According to Euler, the ether is nearly thirty-nine million times thinner than the atmosphere." Our fashionable scientists could give the figures much more exactly if they had a mind to exert their intellects.

Natural philosophers have not yet given to ether all its characteristic marks. But we know that its ultimate particles must be very fine, infinitely smaller than the inconceivably small atoms of matter ; and they creep into all things, even into mathematical points. Ether is found everywhere, filling every nook and corner of space, so that the atoms may have an opportunity to go to work whenever they enter a place. It is a solid, but infinitely more refined than the finest gas. It is either ponderable or imponderable ; if the former, it checks the planets in their course and the comets in their flight ; if the latter, then they move in it without being affected by it, and let the ether pass right through them.

Ether, as far as we now know, has no other mission than to afford the forces of matter a proper medium of communication. Whenever they can get along without the ether it will cease to exist ; but so long as it is needed we shall be perfectly familiar with it, and shall have no difficulty in bestowing on it whatever the forces may require.

Some have been inclined to regard ether as a kind of connecting link between matter and spirit ; but it is wiser to dispense with it altogether than to put it to this use. It is simply a connecting link between matter and matter, or between force and force. Perhaps all the requirements of materialism will be met by making ether a corollary of matter.

Having now given ether (which is matter) to the

atoms of matter, we need only endow them properly and set them to work, a task not more difficult than to find them in the first place. That they have all the properties required to build the universe is a necessary truth ; for how else could they have constructed the cosmos ? Probably only quantity and motion are necessary, which can be measured, while quality cannot ; nevertheless, if future discoveries and inventions prove that difference of quality is needed, it can easily be conferred. If necessary, they can be developed into the monads of Leibnitz, provided they continue to be matter.

I had written the above, and had formed the final conclusion respecting atoms, when I discovered that a new theory had just been proposed which has decided advantages over some others, and is just as reliable. Mr. G. Helm, its author, wrestles boldly with the problem of atoms, of action at a distance, and of ether. He *supposes* the ether to be in all bodies—a conjecture which is very probable ; at least it has never been proved that it is not there ; but I confess to some difficulty in getting it into the atoms, which are so small that they can hardly hold themselves, not to speak of anything else. The gentleman mentioned proposes to overcome all difficulties by depriving matter of everything qualitative, and, as far as I can see, of everything else.* He wants to regard it, not as a substance which moves from place to place, but as a mere condition ; so that in reality we have nothing but motion. " A condition moves from place to place, not matter."

---

* " Vierteljahrsschrift für wissenschaftliche Philosophie." 1882, 4 Heft. 433.

" Matter—namely, ether—continues to exist in various
forms of motion, or, in other words, nothing exists
but different kinds of motion, and possibilities of
motion, in different parts of space. All qualities which
can be ascribed to matter vanish, except the one that
it moves—that is, in the conceptions of ether we need
think of nothing except that which is movable."
Certainly not. But it is best to put this much into
ether, since otherwise it would have absolutely nothing. Respecting atoms, he says : " All is accomplished that is required if one conceives the atom as a
small volume determined by the centre of force sur-
rounding it and filled with ether, which in an atom is
only found in a different condition of density or elas-
ticity from that outside of it." He may have found
the ether in this state in an atom ; but candor obliges
me to admit that I never did. If by this theory " all
is accomplished that is required," it may be regarded
as final until new difficulties arise. As it has motion
without anything that moves, it greatly simplifies
matters.

I think the atoms are now ready for work. Should
any one desire to donate additional attributes to them,
there is no law against his liberality. Being the small-
est and weakest of real and imaginary things, they are
submissiveness itself, and have no power of resistance.
Their repulsive force does not apply to charitable endowments.

The atoms are the " first beginnings" of the universe as well as of Lucretius. Any other co-eternal
existence would endanger philosophical monism.
Pluralism and dualism must be as rigidly excluded
from being as from thought. The astounding per-

fection with which materialism accomplishes this is a confirmation of its truth, and may be regarded as equal to demonstration. With an infinite number of atoms, each separate and distinct, together with their various properties, and with the ether which enables them to work, scientific monism is safe ! The introduction of mind uniting all in one grand purpose, or viewed as the source of all for the accomplishment of some great end, would destroy this monism. Materialism therefore severely excludes intellect. A creative will in and behind all things is a monstrous dualism. Reason cannot be the arbiter in the matter ; and the senses prefer the absolute monism of separate atoms with their properties and with ether.

The atoms simply existed ; they did not know it, nor was anything else aware of the fact. As reason had not yet been born, there was no reason for their existence ; so they existed without reason. There was no reason why they should rest or move, why they should unite or remain separated ; therefore we are privileged to give any reason we please for the conduct we attribute to them. As there was no reason for acting in any other way, they concluded to choose the course finally taken, their action being along the line of least resistance. The law of the conservation of force does not apply to the atoms *per se*, for, as we have already seen, they may have forces at one time which they lack at another, according to emergencies ; but it is in the relation of the atoms to one another that the law applies. By rubbing together, heat was generated ; this heat produced motion, which was again converted into heat. Whether the heat or the motion was first is not material ; whichever came first could easily produce the other. But as there can be no heat without motion, and no motion without heat, both must have acted simultaneously. Motion came first in order that heat might be produced ; and heat came first in order that motion might be possible. Until this juncture of affairs all energy was conserved in a latent form—that is, it was mere force.

In the course of time, a distinction had to be made between the eternity in which the atoms had been at rest, or in motion, and time—in other words, a beginning had to be made. Nothing else could be done until time had been created. This was accomplished by arranging the atoms in a line. All being in a line at once, gave the idea of simultaneousness ; the fact that they followed one another in the line, gave the notion of succession in time ; the different atoms represented the moments ; and by viewing an atom in its relation to those preceding and following, the idea of past, present, and future was obtained. After the completion of time the atoms fell into a heap, which had length, breadth, and thickness, just the idea of space—a fourth dimension not being dreamt of in the infancy of time. This is a natural and intelligent way of accounting for time and space as sensible, but not rational, objects ; and it will readily be accepted by minds made simple enough by the discipline of recent methods and modern faith.

After the creation of time and space, in which all other things exist, the work of creation proceeded rapidly and without interruption. Two or more atoms united to form molecules, and these formed all the chemical compounds. These developed into vegetables, vegetables into animals, animals into men, men

into materialists. But we cannot follow the atoms
through the whole of their creative process, which was
very long, tedious, and laborious. The history of
creation is much better understood than formerly,
since Mr. Haeckel's work on that subject describes a
process which is evidently not the one which that history took. By describing all the other processes which
were not taken, the only one left will be the real instead of the imaginary history.

It is possible that we shall need generous help from
the atoms in the following chapters, in which case
their services will be gratefully accepted. In this one
the sole aim was to secure an exact, definite, lucid,
scientific, atomic basis for materialism, which has now
been accomplished.

CHAPTER V.

EVOLUTION.

" Give me matter, and I will show you how to make a world."
—KANT.
" Evolution is an integration of matter and concomitant dissi-
pation of motion."—SPENCER.

EVOLUTION began at the propitious moment when,
with a simultaneous effort, heat and motion produced
each other. Since that crisis it has continued without interruption, and still retains all the vigor of youth.
As originally the atoms were all alike, but have now
developed into the infinite variety manifest in the
universe, evolution has proceeded from homogeneity
to heterogeneity.

The first unfolding of the tiny atoms made so little
ado that nobody observed it ; but this did not interfere with the process. Modern evolution, however,
depends for success on the applause it receives. But
there are also other differences. Primitive evolution
took place in nature ; the modern occurs in the mind,
and is so superior to the former that it need not take
the natural process into account. Primitive evolution
was therefore natural ; the modern is scientific.
When the latter was born the atoms revealed in its
production a force which till then had been dormant.

It is one of the chief recommendations of modern

evolution that it is so useful and adaptable. Generally that can be evolved which is most desired. It is most scientific to determine first what results are to be attained ; then the facts can be secured and properly shaped. Opposite conclusions may be drawn from the same pliable facts. Indeed, one may gather the facts, while another evolves them into theories, and extracts their abstractions. By stringing together facts and wisely marshalling them, they can be manufactured into forms of society, political institutions, manners and customs, morality and religion. If anything cannot be thus evolved, it has not yet been discovered. Even the social and political future of nations can be foretold. The prophecy may have its effect now ; and when the fulfilment fails to come, the prophecy will likely be forgotten and the prophet safe. For successful evolution, it is better to mass the facts than to subject them to careful criticism and analysis. Reserve respecting hypotheses and prophecies is unscientific.

Primitive man was too much a child of nature to form abstract philosophic notions ; therefore he cannot be regarded as the progenitor of the modern form of the doctrine. The Greeks about the time of Thales began to evolve evolution ; but in spite of their elements and mythologies and mathematics, they were thrown in the shade by the Gnostics of the second century, who were the most expert evolutionists of olden times. With their demiurges and plenty of time they could construct to order anything required. In more recent times Kant and La Place have also evolved the universe, all that they required being a nebula and mathematics, or matter which worked according to certain laws. If matter really took the prescribed course, then their theory was natural as well as philosophical. In still more recent times Schelling and Hegel became eminent evolutionists. The former had genius enough to give a potential philosophy of nature which is independent of nature; and the latter, surpassing all his predecessors, evolved everything from nothing by simply taking the notion of existence and proving that it is the same as that of non-existence. The effort of this same idea of existence and non-existence to balance itself results in a failure; existence falls over into non-existence, and non-existence into existence; and thus things become. If the idea had succeeded in balancing itself, there might never have been any evolution. Mr. Haeckel, as we have already seen, has also exercised his creative talent on the same subject.

But of all evolutionists, ancient and modern, Mr. Herbert Spencer is by far the most celebrated. He reduced modern evolution to a system and gave it laws; and if the process did not follow the prescribed course it is not his fault. The "First Principles" of his system are scattered promiscuously through the first volume of his "Synthetic Philosophy." It is not always apparent which of his opinions are to be taken as *principles*, and which of the principles are *first*, not having been labelled as carefully as mine in the second chapter; it also repeatedly happens that what is stated in one place is contradicted in another; the reader consequently has considerable choice as to which opinions to adopt as principles. The book has many advantages, and is deservedly popular among those whose faith depends on the research and conclusions of others, and I heartily accept it as the final authority on evolution.

Mr. Spencer's method proceeds from the Unknowable to the Knowable, and evolves the latter from the former. He defines the process as follows : " *Evolution is an integration of matter and concomitant dissipation of motion, during which the matter passes from an indefinite, incoherent homogeneity to a definite, coherent heterogeneity, and during which the retained motion undergoes a parallel transformation.*" * This evolution is perfectly intelligible ; it is, according to Mr. Spencer, the only thing we can understand. It is the Known which is evolved from the Unknowable. On page 66 we read : " Force, Space, and Time pass all understanding ;" and he repeatedly states that matter lies wholly beyond the reach of knowledge. The matter integrated and the motion dissipated in evolution, as well as the space and time in which the process occurs, we cannot possibly understand ; but evolution itself is perfectly comprehended, and constitutes the realm in which science delights to revel. The old vulgar method defines the obscure by means of the clear ; the modern profound method defines the obscure by means of the more obscure. That's science.

Having now familiarized ourselves with the secrets of evolution, we can put the atoms through the process. Their first efforts to evolve were by chance, or fate, or accident, or otherwise—design alone being excluded from the region of the possible. After operating for awhile they cultivated habits which became

---

* " First Principles." Third edit. 396.

hereditary, and eventually grew into laws. It is expedient to let the atoms develop their laws, because it
dispenses with a lawgiver. Hume has shown that our
notion of cause is the result of habit ; therefore after
the atoms had acquired fixed habits the effect was
always equal to the cause. We may take it for
granted that even now the law of causality does not prevail in regions where atoms are still in a crude state.
"I am convinced that any one accustomed to abstraction and analysis who will fairly exert his faculties for
the purpose, will, when his imagination has once learned to entertain the notion, find no difficulty in conceiving that in some one, for instance, of the many
firmaments in which sidereal astronomy now divides
the universe, events may succeed one another at ran-
dom, without any fixed law ; nor can anything in our
experience or in our mental nature constitute a sufficient, or indeed any reason for believing that this is
nowhere the case." *

In passing from chance to law, the atoms began
their process of evolution philosophically, for they
passed from the absolutely unknowable chance to
known laws. Since that time the construction of the
universe has been conducted on approved principles.
The laws according to which atoms worked were but
an expression of their nature as developed and disciplined by habit. There was no more choice for
them than there was reason ; and before they had de-

---

* Mill's Logic. First ed., II., 110. I have never had any difficulty in *conceiving* the notion *after* I had entertained it ; my
difficulty has always been in *entertaining* the notion *before* I had
conceived it. But the atoms have not only constituted the minds
of individuals differently, but also work them variously.

veloped themselves into conscience the atoms were
not responsible ; they did what they did simply because they could not do otherwise. Every product
was the result of a necessity as absolute as fate. Probably fate itself was an evolution of chance. They are
opposites in all respects except that they know nothing
about themselves or their work ; and having this element in common, it was, of course, natural for the one
to develop into the other. Fate still reigns supreme,
always excepting such cases as Mr. Mill imagined.
We live in a universe of law. Call the laws physical,
mechanical, chemical, material, or atomic, the slightest deviation in their operation is utterly impossible.
Miracles, if interpreted to mean an interference with
law, never occurred except those hypothetical and
logical ones wrought in our day. This persistence of
blind law inspires confidence in the uniformity and
wisdom of nature ; if the confidence needs it, *law* can
be used in various senses.

Nature is " a blind, insatiable, irresistible fate, . . .
destitute of intelligence and reason, devoid of mercy
and justice." This is no cause for serious regret, for
philosophy can supply the intelligence and reason, and
can evolve mercy and justice enough from brutes.
To speak of the possibilities of nature is absurd, for
there are none. All is wrapped in the steel bands of
necessity, and is controlled by stern, severe, adaman-
tine force, whose absolute certainty is without an ink-
ling of choice or possibility. As soon as law began
its work of fate, all that was to come to pass throughout the ages of eternity was irresistibly and irrevocably
fixed—without intelligence, without reason, without
choice, without mercy, without justice ; and at that

moment a good mathematician could have worked out the future problems of the universe. He might have foretold every change of the weather, could have traced the course of every bullet at the battle of Waterloo, and might even have hit some of the conclusions of modern natural philosophy.

There is nothing on which we materialists insist more strenuously than on this absolute and infinite necessity as the controlling factor in evolution. It is a fundamental axiom of our thoughts, and from it we get valuable necessary truths. All that exists in any way or anywhere is the direct and sole product of the blind forces of matter; and we are determined that nothing else shall be smuggled into the universe. Fate is the Reason of materialism ; and whatever it cannot explain is either not worthy of explanation, or may be referred to that " mysterious thing" which explains everything, or to the " Unknowable" which evolves evolution.

Mr. Huxley* says : " The whole analogy of natural operations furnishes so complete and crushing an argument against the intervention of any but what are termed secondary causes, in the production of all the phenomena of the universe, that, in view of the intimate relations between man and the rest of the living world, and between the forces exerted by the latter and all other forces, I can see no excuse for doubting that all are co-ordinated terms of nature's great progression, from the formless to the formed, from the inorganic to the organic, from blind force to conscious intellect and will." Philosophy is, in fact, obliged to

* " Man's Place in Nature," 108.

take this position, for it would be lamentable weakness to admit that its investigations are limited to "natural operations" and "secondary causes" if anything else exists in the world. Nowhere does modern philosophy discover a First Cause or supernatural operations ; and if it did, it would not know what to do with them. The "natural operations" are perfectly understood, their factors being the absolutely mysterious matter and force. The "secondary causes" are just as fully comprehended as "all the phenomena of the universe" produced by them. "Nature's great progression" and its "co-ordinated forces" are objects with which we are intimately familiar. What astounding wisdom is disclosed in revelations of the Unknowable by means of phrases so profound that their analysis lands one in the abyss of nothing !

Nature's great progression "from blind force to conscious intellect and will" is of more than ordinary interest. The inconceivable evolves the conceivable ; the formless, the formed ; the inorganic, the organic ; the blind evolves sight ; the unconscious, consciousness ; necessity, freedom—in other words, everything unfolds itself into its opposite. The physical forces are co-ordinated with the mental, and pass over the physical into the mental. Consciousness is as much a product of physical force as motion is, and the same is true of reason, conscience, and will. Bright hopes are in fact cherished that all these will soon be reduced to motion. With unfathomable wisdom heat has been called "simply structureless intelligence." After long and laborious effort to explain this conception of heat I found it self-evident.

Mental phenomena are no obstacles at all in the way of materialists. With his usual refinement and exquisite taste, Professor Carl Vogt declares "that thought is related to the brain as gall to the liver or urine to the kidneys." Long before this classic utterance it was suspected that thought is only a secretion of the brain, or a product of the rubbing of the molecules of matter, or of some other equally intelligible and demonstrable process ; but the scientific formula was not found until the Zurich professor put daylight into the evolution of thought.

Some spiritualist might indeed imagine that matter reaches its limits before it creates the mental processes, and that consequently there are phenomena which are not material. But is it not one of the principles of materialism that there is nothing but matter in the universe ? And what is a system worth if it is not true to its principles ? Professor Bain, in his book on "Mind and Body," referring to Mr. Robert Hook, says : "In his lectures upon Light, he makes ideas to be material substances, and thinks that the brain is furnished with a proper kind of matter, for fabricating the ideas of each sense. The ideas of sight, he thinks, are formed of a kind of matter resembling the Bononian stone, or some kind of phosphorus." This shows a striking familiarity with the subject, and is undoubtedly the correct view. Like always produces like ; consequently matter always produces matter ; hence ideas are of course material. All that is necessary is "the proper kind of matter"—that is, matter which is able to do all that is required. In Erasmus Darwin's "Zoonomia" the word *Idea* "is defined a contraction, a motion, a configuration of the

fibres which constitute the immediate organs of
sense ;" "our *ideas* are animal motions of the organ
of sense."

In this way philosophy demonstrates that physical
become mental laws, that matter becomes mind, and
that motion becomes thought. Since the physical
laws work with a blind necessity, all their products are
fixed, necessary, and absolutely certain. They never
can make a mistake. All that exists—call it matter or
mind or motion or thought—is produced by them. To-
day these necessary laws evolve one view, and to-morrow the same necessary laws produce its opposite in the
same mind. The one is just as necessary as the other,
and just as reliable : what is absolutely necessary must
also be absolutely certain. Every superstition is the
product of these unvarying and necessary laws, from
the lowest fetichism to the sublimest spirituality.
These physical laws created the infernal systems which
have cursed the world, and evolved the religious
abominations which so justly arouse the ire of materialists and furnish thunder for the eloquence of certain
historians ; they developed the horrors of the Span-
ish Inquisition, and invented instruments of torture
whose very sight makes the flesh creep ; they burned
every martyr, and committed every crime which is a
foul blot on history's page ; and the physical laws not
only did these things, but it was absolutely necessary to
do them. The superstitions at which Voltaire sneered
and which Buckle and others censure are the result of
" nature's great progression," and are as much the pure
product of matter as motion itself. There are no degrees in necessity ; the burning of Huss and Servetus
was as much a physical necessity as the fall of an unsup-

ported weight to the earth. Censure, blame, curses? They simply fall on matter and its laws, unless a man chooses to be a fool as well as a materialist. Materialism never blinks. Whatever is necessary is right. Every murder ever committed was unavoidably necessary, and was as directly the consequence of matter and its laws as is the movement of the tides ; and of course it was just as right. Herod and Nero and modern assassins and villains, steeped in the foulest corruption, are as pure as the most spotless saints that ever trod the earth. Their villainy was just as physical and just as unavoidable as the saintly purity. There are no demons or fiends, just as there are no ghosts. Heroes are myths ; they could not help being heroes, just as the cowards are cowards from a material necessity ; and both are equally meritorious. There are no crimes ; there are no virtues ; both belong to mythology. The deed called hellish deserves a monument just as much as that called divine ; and both as much as the wolf for devouring his prey or the hog for wallowing in the mire. Materialism is the great leveller, and never blinks. What is necessary must be true ; for necessity cannot produce a lie. The effect must always equal the cause ; if, then, the cause is a blind necessity, so must its product be, and both if necessary must also be reliable and true. Can one imagine necessary physical laws producing anything false ? If they could, where would be the truth of science ? Therefore the opposite views of conflicting systems ; the *yes* of faith and the *no* of unbelief ; the assurance of yesterday, the doubt of to-day, and the denial of to-morrow ; the doctrine of theism and of atheism, of materialism and idealism, and all other conflicting views are equally reliable and true, all being the direct product of the same physical necessity.

We materialists are not such idiots as to suppose that a necessary law ceases to be necessary after the physical forces have been transmuted into the mental. When ignorant men denounce religion as superstition, crime as criminal, and abominations as abominable, they forget that they are simply slandering matter. I cannot imagine why Vogt and Büchner get so terribly angry at the men who oppose their theories, after they have reduced everything to matter and force and their laws. Their own theory is that these opponents were forced to oppose them; why, then, work themselves into an insane fury because the natural laws force matter to operate as it does in their antagonists? But the whole is explained when we remember that their own wrath is also the direct and necessary product of matter and its laws, and the poor fellows cannot help themselves!

In the process of evolution matter becomes mind, and the physical is transformed into the spiritual. All that exists is the product of necessity; but man is conscious of freedom; therefore the consciousness of freedom is a necessity. All that man is and thinks and feels is a necessity; therefore all moral and immoral character, all lies and deceptions and mistakes and false hopes, are a necessity.

Since matter is evolved into spirit, it is evident that the spiritual is material. If there is nothing but matter, of course mind and spirit are matter; they are simply matter in a peculiar form or in a peculiar motion. It would be absurd to suppose that matter ceases to be matter after it becomes spirit. Matter is

therefore spirit, and the material is spiritual. Materialism is, therefore, spiritual as well as material, and thus
it is evident that we are justified in choosing our title—
Spiritual Materialism.

But if the physical and mental forces are so corre-
lated that they are really one and the same, and if
they can be transmuted into each other, why not
begin with mind, and thence proceed to matter, instead
of proceeding from matter to mind ? In this way it
could be shown that an idea is changed into a volition,
that the volition affects the nerves and muscles, and
that thus the mental are transmuted into physical
forces. Instead of making the mental an evolution of
the material, the process would be reversed, and the
material forces would be shown to be a product of the
mental. Men naturally begin with their minds, for
they (materialists alone excepted) get all the ideas
there, and know force only through their mind. As
Principal Caird says, " You cannot get mind as an
ultimate product of matter, for in the very attempt to
do so you have already begun with mind." Although
Lotze passed from medicine to philosophy, he says :
" Of all the mistakes made by the human mind, this
has always seemed to me the strangest : that it could
question its own existence, of which alone it is immediately conscious, or could regard itself as a product of external nature, which we know only second-
hand, only through the knowledge mediated by the
mind whose existence we denied." If, however,
men like Caird and Lotze would develop their minds
less, and matter more, they would experience no
difficulty in losing themselves in external things. The
more intensely conscious of self, of mind, of spirit a

man becomes, the more he unfits himself for consistent materialism ; but he who loses his mind as well as his senses in matter finds it easy to make matter mind, though he may never have the mind to evolve the mental into the material.   The thorough materialist, after getting the idea of matter furnished by the mind, drops the mind and hugs the matter.

Since the material forces are the mental, why not, then, begin with the latter and proceed from the mental to the physical ?   One way is just about as reliable as the other, but they are not equally expedient.   If we begin at one end we resolve all into matter and physical forces, and the result is a materialism which ends in idealism and spiritualism ; and if we begin at the other end we have mind and mental forces as the starting-point, and the result is an idealism which ends in materialism.   Mr. Spencer* says :   " Men who have not risen above the vulgar conception which unites with matter the contemptuous epithets ' gross ' and ' brute ' may naturally feel dismay at the proposal to reduce the phenomena of Life, of Mind, and of Society to a level with those which they think so degraded.   But whoever remembers that the forms of existence which the uncultivated speak of with so much scorn are shown by the man of science to be the more marvellous in their attributes the more they are investigated, and are also proved to be in their ulti- mate natures absolutely incomprehensible—as abso- lutely incomprehensible as sensation, or the conscious something which perceives it—whoever clearly recog- nizes this truth, will see that the course proposed does

* " First Principles," 556.

not imply a degradation of the so-called higher, but an elevation of the so-called lower. Perceiving as he will that the materialist and spiritualist controversy is a mere war of words, in which the disputants are equally absurd, each thinking he understands that which it is impossible for any man to understand, he will perceive how utterly groundless is the fear referred to. Being fully convinced that whatever nomenclature is used the ultimate mystery must remain the same, he will be as ready to formulate all phenomena in terms of matter, motion, and force as in any other terms, and will rather indeed anticipate that only in a doctrine which recognizes the Unknown Cause as co-extensive with all orders of phenomena can there be a consistent religion or a consistent philosophy."

He also says : " The materialist, seeing it to be a necessary deduction from the law of correlation that what exists in consciousness under the form of feeling is transformable into an equivalent of mechanical motion, and by consequence into equivalents of all the other forces which matter exhibits, may consider it therefore demonstrated that the phenomena of consciousness are material phenomena. But the spiritualist, setting out with the same data, may argue with equal cogency that if the forces displayed by matter are cognizable only under the shape of those equivalent amounts of consciousness which they produce, it is to be inferred that these forces, when existing out of consciousness, are of the same intrinsic nature as when existing in consciousness ; and that so is justified the spiritualistic conception of the external world, as consisting of something essentially identical with what we call mind. Manifestly, the establishment of correlation

and equivalence between the forces of the outer and
the inner worlds may be used to assimilate either to
the other, according as we set out with one or the
other term."

A refined view of matter and not too refined a view
of spirit will enable us to accomplish wonders. But
why not begin with mind, and thus reduce all to
mental and spiritual laws ? Why adopt the materialist
view instead of the spiritualist, since both are equally
true ? You will have the animal whether you catch
it by the head or the tail ; and the distance from the
one to the other is the same, whether you begin to
measure at one end or at the other ; of course it is all
the same which is viewed as head, which as tail,
provided both are held as well as all that lies between.
At which end we begin is purely a matter of taste ;
whether we use the head to interpret the tail or the
tail to interpret the head is not essential. Looked at
carefully, good reasons may be found for preferring
to begin with matter. It is palpable ; we see, touch,
handle, weigh, measure it ; we have an immediate
and perfect knowledge of it ; while of mind we know
little or nothing, and that vaguely, obscurely. Therefore that we begin with matter is material, and that
we begin with spirit is immaterial.

I was casting about for other reasons for beginning
with matter, when Professor Ferrier's invincible reasoning, as quoted by Professor Bain, met my eye :
" In vain does the spiritualist found an argument for
the existence of a separate immaterial substance on the
alleged incompatibility of the intellectual and physical
phenomena to co-inhere in the same substratum.
Materiality may well stand the brunt of that unshotted

broadside. This mild artifice can scarcely expect to
be treated as a serious observation. Such an hypothesis cannot be meant to be in earnest. Who is to
dictate to nature what phenomena or what qualities
inhere in what substances—what effects may result
from what causes? Matter is already in the field as
an acknowledged entity—this both parties admit.
Mind, considered as an independent entity, is not so
unmistakably in the field. Therefore, as entities are
not to be multiplied without necessity, we are not
entitled to postulate a new cause, so long as it is
possible to account for the phenomena by a cause
already in existence—which possibility has never yet
been disproved.''

This, I rejoice to say, settles the question scientifically. '' Matter is already in the field,'' and, as everybody knows, possession is nine points in law. '' Who
is to dictate to nature?'' That's what we'd like to
know. We do not even know what it can produce ;
how, then, can we dictate what it cannot? No one
has ever demonstrated that matter cannot do everything, nor is it likely that any one ever will ; and so
long as this is not done, it may be regarded as settled
that matter can accomplish everything. The *possibility*
has never been proved an impossibility ; therefore it
is a possibility still. Thus even the most superficial
thought and the shallowest reasoning dictate that a
beginning should be made with matter. But the most
potent reason is still to be given : if we begin with
mind materialism will be endangered. If the mental
can pass over into physical forces, how do we know
that, after all, the physical forces in nature are not
only the same as those in our minds, but also the prod-

uct of mind ? How do we know then that, after all,
some idea does not lie behind matter ? We know that
the physical forces pass right over into the mental ;
but the confusion would be intolerable if the mental
forces were to become physical. Then mind might
come first ; then there might be reason before the
atoms had evolved it ; then there might be a lawgiver
and a —God where they are not wanted. No, no, it
is safer not to begin with the mental powers. Our
principle of the humility of materialism makes it necessary to stick to the lowest and make it the interpreter
of the highest.

Materialism thus beautifully meets all objections.
When it is argued that matter is extended, but that
thought and spirit are not extended, and therefore are
not matter, the reasoning is absurd. If the physical
forces in becoming mental can divest themselves
wholly of their physical properties and reveal new
ones which are nowhere discovered where physical
forces are known to exist, I do not see why matter,
which must be extended in order to be what we understand by matter, cannot wholly lose its extension in
passing over into spirit and thought.

If necessary, take Professor Bain's view—" The
one substance, with two sets of properties, two sides,
the physical and the mental—*a double-faced unity*—
would appear to comply with all the exigencies of the
case." Two sets of properties ? Take a score if
necessary, provided that the substance properly endowed continues to be matter. If anything else is
needed, take the view of Professor Clifford, that
" mind-stuff is the reality which we perceive as matter." Whether the thing is conceivable or not, we at

least have "stuff," and that savors sufficiently of matter not to be seriously offensive. He says : "A moving molecule of inorganic matter does not possess mind or consciousness, but it possesses a small piece of mind-stuff. When molecules are so combined together as to form the film on the under side of a jelly-fish, the elements of mind-stuff which go along with them are so combined as to form the faint beginnings of sentience. When the molecules are so combined as to form the brain and nervous system of a vertebrate, the corresponding elements of mind-stuff are so combined as to furnish same kind of consciousness. . . . When matter takes the complex form of a living human brain, the corresponding mind-stuff takes the form of human consciousness, having intelligence and volition." I have no doubt that if this "mind-stuff" really exists, and if its properties could be discovered, it would be of incalculable service to evolution.

These are only hints as to the courses which may be taken if difficulty is experienced in evolving mind from matter. If these are not entirely satisfactory, some other method can be found. But the principal desideratum is neither evolution of mind from matter nor the explanation of the operation ; the essential thing is the establishment of the fact that this is the way mind is produced, which has been stated so frequently that all reasonable persons ought now to be convinced.

Interesting as it is to trace evolution from the "first beginnings" to the present, it is not less so to cast a prophetic glance into the future and inquire into the next stages and the final result of the process. This subject being freed from the bondage of facts is one over which modern genius hovers with

delight. The final result will no doubt be sublime.
It may be that those philosophers are right who regard
the entire process of evolution as a development of the
Divine Being—that is, a process which constantly
tends to produce Him, though it never fully accomplishes its object.   Much is gained by relegating Him
beyond reach, at the end which is never attained, instead of putting Him at the beginning and then continuing Him forever.   In the profoundest science that
is always last which is first, and that is first which is
last.

We are accustomed to speak of man as the final product of evolution.   But *final* is here taken in the
modern scientific sense—namely, the final of to-day
may be the beginning of a new series to-morrow.   By
means of our wonderful powers of prevision modern
philosophy can determine just what processes of evolution will occur in the future.   From the sum of all
the possible powers of matter we simply subtract those
which have already been exerted ; the result is the
powers which will work in the future.   In this way
the problem is reduced to a simple sum in arithmetic.
A mere outline of future evolution must here suffice.

If matter has not exhausted its resources in producing man, it may yet evolve something as much superior to him as the present lord of creation is to
the atoms—something neither vegetable, animal, nor
human.   But this something may have to wait a long
time before it is evolved ; at any rate, we are more intensely interested in the new creature to be evolved
immediately from man.   The unscientific members of
the human family can form no more conception of the
new race which is to emerge from it than the ape

could of man before he made his appearance ; and the
ordinary man will no more be able to appreciate the
new race after it appears than the monkey can estimate
man after associating with him. The new evolvement
will be allied to our conception of angels, except that
it (or he) will be purely material ; it will be as superior
to man as the deductive is to the inductive scientist.
We can the more accurately describe the coming being
because forerunners thereof have already appeared.

The new descendant of man will be an originalist.
Gifted intuitively with an inside knowledge of matter, he will instinctively understand all its properties,
and will determine *a priori* all it can do. Being too
cultured to believe, he will only know ; and the first
axiom of his science will be that there are no spirits
(which is synonymous with ghosts), but that spirit is
matter. He will of course not be a scientist of the
old school, but of the modern type. His vivid imagination and lively fancy will be capable of astounding
feats, and from the hot-bed of his brain theories will
grow naturally and luxuriantly like weeds. Only they
can solve the problems of the world who see with his
eyes. He will not study history, but will regard
Greek culture and Christian civilization much as we
do the culture of a family of apes. No emotion can
ever agitate him, since he will have neither heart nor
soul ; freed from all superstition, he will not be religious, nor will he comprehend how any one can be ;
he will be a stranger to the torments of conscience,
and his morality, if he has any, will be purely pleasurable. After the first generation or two science will
become instinctive. It is self-evident that as a thorough materialist he will find no difficulty in following

the atoms through their motions till they produced
him.   The principles of our second chapter will be the
laws of his wisdom.

Whenever man is ready he will evolve this new
species or genus.   It may appear at any time ; but
however sudden the evolvement, it will hardly cause
astonishment, since man has now been forewarned, and
can prepare himself to become the ape of the new
race.   After this race is born, all the links between it
and man will vanish forever—that's the law—leaving
the human family and the new lord of creation related
to each other as distinct species.   By a careful comparison of some of their characteristics it will, however, be found that in the new race there are greater
differences than between that race and man ; and in
this way it will be possible to demonstrate that the
new family is a descent from humanity.

In course of time this genus will become the ancestor of a still greater race, differing from itself as
much as it does from man.   After it has been successfully evolved, the connecting links will disappear ;
but that will be no loss, since the imagination can
supply them.   Then another new species will be
evolved, then another, and so on indefinitely until the
powers of matter are exhausted.   But it is not probable that they will ever be exhausted ; in their unfolding they may continually develop new possibilities,
so that every new and greater product will only prepare for a still newer and a still greater one.   But if
a highest possible product of matter is ever evolved, it
will be so immeasurably superior to man that it will
hardly be possible to institute a comparison.   That
ultimate will neither be conscious nor unconscious, but

something infinitely more exalted ; it will neither be personal nor impersonal, neither rational nor irrational ; it will simply be what is now known as the Unknowable. It will be the infinite, absolute product of matter—the crowning glory of spiritual materialism.

Then retrogression will start—that is, the highest will produce the next lower, that another lower form, and so on until matter again lands in the atoms. Then the work of evolution will begin anew, and the whole process will have to be gone over again. This evolution and reversion will be eternal ; indeed, it has already been going on forever. It may be that we are now on the back track, and that man is not at all the product of apes, but a descent from a race more glorious than himself. If this is the correct view, then the forerunners of the new race mentioned above are the lingering fragments of man's noble ancestors. But whether the sprouts of a coming genus or the tail of a vanishing one, advanced materialists are earth's choicest sons.

The ape, instead of being man's father, may be his child ; and instead of looking for a higher being than man to spring from evolution, it may be that the human family will soon disappear altogether, and that the ape will be the sole lord of creation. However that may be, there are strong tendencies which, if successful, will sponge out all the qualitative differences between man and his simian progenitor or descendant.

CHAPTER VI.

DESIGN.

" Overpowering proof of intelligence and benevolent design lie all around us ; and if ever perplexities, whether metaphysical or scientific, turn us away from them for a time, they come back upon us with irresistible force, showing to us through nature the influence of a free will, and teaching us that all living beings depend upon one ever-acting Creator and Ruler."—SIR WILLIAM THOMSON.

I HASTEN to apologize for not disposing of design long ago ; but by means of the delay the way has been the more thoroughly prepared for proving that it does not exist. Indeed, whoever has pondered the preceding arguments and been convinced by them is already in the right frame of mind to need no more proof ; but minds like the one quoted at the head of this chapter are not so easily satisfied. The following will, however, demonstrate to them that through nature we see only the vibrations of the atoms, and not " the influence of a free will."

It is one of the advantages of beginning and ending with matter that it logically dispenses with design in nature, which is rather hard to get rid of when one begins with mind. That is the difficulty with metaphysicians : they view everything in a mental and rational light, and therefore are haunted by intelligence and design. But the materialist avoids all perplexities by stepping out of his mind into matter.

DESIGN.

99

Quite an advantage will be gained by again determining beforehand just what a thing must be and do,
if we are to admit purpose in its construction. After
this has been settled it becomes evident that whatever
other purpose there may be in it, we can reject all
evidence of design, just because it does not comply
with our conditions. For instance, if we determine
that intelligence can be manifested only in what is perfect according to our conception, then wherever we
think we discover imperfection there is conclusive
proof against design. How can there be reason behind things, when, even with our perfect insight into
the universe, we fail to discover it? If there were any
intelligence in or behind matter it would have to be
so universal and so apparent that anything discovered
in which we see no intelligent purpose must be proof
that even where seen it must be interpreted as something else than design.

The matter is thus simplified by making the failure
to find design in any one thing the proof that there is
none anywhere. The fact that in a million things we
see no design would not convince some minds of the
correctness of our position ; for they might say that it
may be there, even if we fail to discover it. And if in
a single case design could be incontrovertibly established, some persons would regard it as evidence that
there is intelligence and design in nature. Therefore
it is essential to wipe out all traces of the kind everywhere, and to insist that it must be something else.

Rightly considered, it is self-evident that there can
be no design in nature ; for that is something mental,
and there is nothing of the kind in matter, at least not
before it has evolved mind. Kant saw that design is

intellectual, and that the mind in attributing it to things really projects itself into nature. Now, it is well known that nature is the more perfectly comprehended the less mind is projected into its phenomena. Matter passes into mind, not mind into matter—that's the scientific rule.

Probably we can best get rid of design by resolving to make it a necessary truth that there is none ; but it can also be demonstrated that there can be none. With his usual acumen, Mr. Büchner begins his argument against design by stating that we have no means for its recognition. " How can we speak of conformity to an end, since we know things only in this one shape and form, and have no idea how they would appear to us in any other shape or form ?" After stating that we could not recognize it if it existed, he proceeds to search for proofs against its existence. A vulgar logic would conclude that if we have not the means of recognizing design, then we cannot argue on the subject ; but a modern scientist proves that we can know nothing about design, and then demonstrates that there can be none ! With the same author, we fearlessly assert : " Nature knows neither intention nor design nor any spiritual or material conditions forced on it from without or from above. It has developed itself out of itself organically from beginning to end, and continues to develop itself ceaselessly."

This view is confirmed by Lucretius, who held that there is no plan or purpose whatever in the movement of the atoms. By knocking one another about eternally they pass by chance through all possible motions and combinations until they happen into the present order. After finding themselves in this position, their tendency is somehow to maintain and develop the beautiful system formed accidentally after various experiments. Probably the existing order has continued so long as now to be a fixed habit. But there is no guarantee that things will not fall apart again accidentally into chaos. That faith which builds on the fortuitous concourse of the atoms needs more props than Lucretius and his followers give, in order to secure it against future accidents. A single atom out of joint might wreck the universe. But this does not affect the scientific character of the theory, for the future stability of the cosmos is only a postulate of the imagination ; and even if false it does not overthrow the essential element in the doctrine of Lucretius— namely, that things have become what they are without design. The grand consummation of all things may be their total destruction. Strauss may be right— " Then all living and rational beings, and all labors and performances of these beings, all political institutions, all works of art and science, will not only have disappeared without leaving a trace of themselves, but there will not even be left the memory of them in any mind" —there will be no mind to remember. The end of things will thus be worthy of their beginning.

Darwin, with Haeckel's comments and even leadership, is of immense service for the proper interpretation of evidences of intelligence. Although " natural selection" is still an hypothesis, there is no doubt that it will be firmly established in the future ; even now those who heartily adopt all its conclusions have no difficulty in regarding it as a demonstrated fact or law. In the " struggle for existence" on the part of plants and animals, those of course gain the victory which are best adapted to their environment or are best fitted to live. This is the law of the "survival of the fittest," or it is natural selection, nature selecting for preservation those which are fittest. The fittest transmit their favorable characteristics to their descendants, according to the law of heredity, and thus the succeeding generations grow in their adaptations to their environment. Since only the fittest live and transmit their qualities, those plants and animals which have been transmitting for a while are now perfect, and have no weak or defective offspring.

Just how natural selection works we do not understand, and what it accomplishes we do not know. There are other causes, as Mr. Darwin freely admits. "I am convinced that natural selection has been the most important, but not the exclusive means of modification." Even natural selection leaves a few mysteries. "No one ought to feel surprise at much remaining as yet unexplained in regard to the origin of species and varieties, if he make due allowance for our perfect ignorance in regard to the mutual relations of the many beings which live around us."* This reserve is very unfortunate ; but those who are the heirs of his views have not been prevented from developing and applying them so as to help materialism. In the same volume he leaves room for design and a Creator, and sorrowfully we read at its close these words : "To my mind it accords better with what we know of the laws impressed on matter by the Creator, that the production and extinction of the past and present inhabit-

---

* "Origin of Species." Introduction.

ants of the world should have been due to secondary causes, like those determining the birth and death of the individual. . . . There is grandeur in this view of life, with its several powers, having been originally breathed by the Creator into a few forms or into one." Here a Creator is superstitiously recognized, and the laws of matter are viewed as his work ; thus design is still admitted, though pushed back out of the way as far as possible. Perhaps in later years the leader overcame the superstitions which his best followers have long ago rejected.

But we are not confined to natural selection. We can add sexual selection, affinities, correlation of forces, habit, impulse, tendency to development, adaptations, heredity, and whatever else is required. Any one of these may be made a general law, and then the others can be viewed as subordinate. They can be so manipulated as to banish from them all evidence of rational intelligence. Theologians and metaphysicians may claim that some of these terms sadly need explanation ; but we do not introduce these terms to explain them, but for the sake of explaining other things.

Indeed, it strikes me that natural selection itself beautifully disposes of all design in nature. If an animal can transmute itself into harmony with its surroundings the question is settled. An intelligent Creator could never have thought of making living beings which can so change as to adapt themselves to their environment. He would have made the types so rigid that with a change of environment the animals must perish, and the creation of new types would become necessary. To view natural selection itself, and the laws supposed to work in it, as evidence of design would be monstrous !

Something may be gained by directing the attention as much as possible from the things themselves to their conditions, and to invest these conditions with the needed requirements. Motion may be treated abstractly, without wasting time in contemplating the thing moved. This adds profundity to the investigation. A point will also be gained if originally the motion can be made to start itself, and can somehow, through some inherent power, direct itself and determine its course. When the wonderful transforming power of things is to be shown, it is not necessary to prove that the existing form has in it the conditions for developing, without additions, the thing we want to evolve ; nor is it necessary to give examples of the real transformation ; it is only required to assume limitless time and other conditions which lie beyond the reach of observation and investigation. Who will prove that the transformation did not occur in that way ? However little the causes working in natural selection may be understood, he is miserly who will not grant them the privilege of doing everything without foreign intervention. Speaking of the causes working in natural selection, Mr. John Fiske asks that only the following be granted : " It is postulated that, since the first appearance of life upon the earth's surface, sufficient time has elapsed to have enabled such causes as the foregoing to produce all the specific heterogeneity now witnessed." Time can do it, of course, and it would be mean not to give the theory all it needs. The character of the thing to be evolved into the heterogeneity need not be considered. There is much mystery in the matter—that is admitted on all hands ; for that very reason we claim the privilege of taking it for granted that time alone, and enough of it, is all that is required. Mystery is an invincible stronghold.

How grand the cosmos after eliminating design ! Nature is a marvellous mechanism, working with a harmony that is astounding ; it is a machine without a mechanist. Like Topsy, it just grew. Helmholtz declares that all mechanism is the result of intelligence ; but how any got into the universe, since there is none at its basis or behind it, is inexplicable, unless we view mind as a development of matter. All this reason and harmony, without intention and without reason, is nothing short of a miracle. The marvel would cease if a Being of limitless intelligence and power had constructed the universe. But to view it in all its sublimity as without a Creator, as evolving itself without knowing it, as developing reason in man and the correspondences with it in nature, as adapting its objects so perfectly without intention, is well calculated to fill the mind with wonder and reverence. With such a miracle before us we can afford to dispense with the vanished and vanishing myths and superstitions of the past.

There is perfect operation of law without a lawgiver. Had there been a lawgiver, where would be the mystery such as religion needs for its very life ? But without this lawgiver we find in law that mystery, that twilight, that starless midnight, in which religion revels and breathes its sanctified atmosphere. Only one thing more is required to make religion perfect, and that, too, is found—a nature stern and merciless, which

adds to the painful mystery a dread for which there is
no relief.*

Law itself, with its perfect regularity and working
toward an end, has been viewed as an expression of
intelligence ; but a modern philosophic inventor has
discovered that where it prevails intellect is excluded.
Thus design is banished from nature in which law
reigns. The watch works according to law, and what
more is needed ? Newton, though living in the infancy of science, taught that hypotheses should not be
unnecessarily multiplied ; and recently it has been
discovered that this rule makes intelligence useless.
A machine which works according to a certain plan is
of itself all sufficient, and intellect would be a superfluity. From the fire which boils the water, to the
revolutions of the wheels in the machinery of a great
factory, and to the work performed thereby, there is
not an iota of intellect. Intelligence need only step
in when the machinery is imperfect and wants repairs ;
but the mechanism of the universe has so constructed
itself that it never gets out of repair, never makes a
mistake, and consequently never needs intelligence.
The same is true of a state : only when its laws are
imperfect or do not work right is it necessary for mind
to interfere. Haeckel, who is an authority on the
subject, has added some original matter on this point ;
and we may regard it as settled by him that just as a
perfect machine and perfect laws of a state are devoid
of mind, so the laws of the universe are so perfect as
to exclude every suggestion of intelligence.

This demonstration is based on the supposition that

* Timor fecit deos.

the laws developed themselves, or that the things
developed them as they grew up from the atoms and
formed their habits. But the same result is obtain-
able, and the proof will be just as reliable, if we exclude all inquiry into the origin of the laws. It is, in
fact, much better to avoid such investigations, since
questions respecting origin and tendency distract, confuse, and worry, and are apt to suggest action with a
definite end in view. When we succeed in excluding
from our idea of law every suggestion of intelligence,
as well as every question respecting its source and end,
we are not likely to be troubled with design.

By this time it has probably become sufficiently
evident that there can be no purpose in the universe.
The demonstration will be still more conclusive if we
confine our thoughts to the laws working *blindly.*
And how else could they work ? Evidently a law has
no foresight, no plan, no aim ; it accomplishes its
work simply because it cannot help itself. From this
it is evident that there are various ways of viewing law
without intellect.

Persons not philosophically trained might claim that
of course there can be no design in nature, since it belongs to mind only ; but that in nature there are *evidences* of design, while the design itself is found in
the author of nature. But we have long ago settled
it that nature has no author. Besides, this distinction
between design and its evidences confuses the subject
and introduces problems which should be rigidly excluded.

This demonstration leads me to remark that for consistent thought and the attainment of the desired results it is a good rule not to go back too far for the

ultimate cause, nor to peer very far into the future to
inquire into effects.   Let things be examined individ-
ually rather than in their relation to other objects or
to the totality of existence.   One thing can be better
managed than many, and relations are extremely difficult, and might prove risky.   While the senses are
open and the mind shut there is very little danger of
going astray.   As long as we weigh and measure we
are not likely to discover intelligence, which is not subject to such tests ; but when we yield to reflection, the
thought of the purpose and reason of things will obtrude
itself ; and even those who know that there are no
evidences of design in nature are continually using
language which implies that there are such evidences.
But with one blow the question respecting final causes
can be settled by making the atoms themselves these
causes.   Things probably had a cause, and that cause
must have been sufficient to account for the all that
exists ; but unless we give the atoms this place, we
may, by reasoning from effect to cause, at last find
what can neither be weighed nor measured.   The
same is true of questions respecting the tendency of
things ; they involve us in endless contradictions and
absurdities.   The very word *tendency* has a flavor of
design, and it is better to demonstrate that things have
no tendency.   He who inquires into the source, the
reason, and consummation of all things deals with
subjects which imply intellect, and which are apt to
lead one to lose sight of present realities and to put
the rational for the sensible—always a precarious proceeding.   Above all, questions respecting the aim of
man, the longing and aspiration of his soul, the power
and intuitions of his spirit, are irrelevant after it has

been shown that there is no intellect in nature, of which man is a part.

These suggestions are the more necessary because even Du Bois-Reymond, who recognizes no deity, cannot explain the evidences of design in nature. And von Hartmann everywhere sees the most striking evidences of intellect, though he nowhere sees a God. So deeply is he impressed by these evidences that he puts behind nature the *Unconscious*, with reason and will. While reading his " Philosophy of the Unconscious" the impression gradually grows on the mind that its author regards him as devoid of intellect who cannot see it in nature. That he could not get rid of intellect after he got rid of God shows how essential it is not to let the mind wander beyond the guidance of the senses. If something beyond these is needed, take the atoms, make them omnipotent, and thus " circumvent God."

This must be done, or materialism is doomed. It is not a question of special creation or of interference with law that concerns us. God put anywhere as a reality endangers the supremacy of matter, and this is a violation of the first commandment of materialism. Put God ever so far back, it still makes matter but the glass through which the light of the divine intellect falls upon us. This would extricate us from design with a vengeance—namely, by showing that the divine mind directs all things, and that the final result must be in harmony with His purposes. A God behind matter and law ! Then all discrepancies may be only apparent, and conflicts and miseries may be but links in the chain of progress forged by time in its onward march and tending to that final consummation of all things which the Deity has in view. In this way apparent evidences against design would only prove that we are too short-sighted to discern the end from the beginning. Then law would be but the embodiment of thought and plan and purpose ; the universe would be radiant with the light of reason ; and matter and force would be marshalled by intellect, and would serve a purpose. The unity thus attained is painfully perfect, and so rational that it is at once stamped as a product of the erring reason, and not of the sure senses. This process of reasoning is annihilated by Mr. Büchner's fatal objection that it is a product of the " reflecting understanding," while his design is " the necessary result of the meeting of natural substances and forces."

With the most honest effort to get rid of intelligence and design in nature, we wrestle with difficulties which at times seem insurmountable, as some have probably felt while reading this argument. The reason is plain, and by fathoming it we shall succeed in overcoming even these difficulties. The mind sees in nature evidences of working similar to its own ; and it naturally judges the processes of nature as it would similar ones in itself. Looking into the mirror of nature, it everywhere recognizes reflections of its own ideas and purposes. The reason in things is in harmony with the reason in the mind, addresses it, and reveals itself as its affinity. This renders it almost impossible to speak intelligently of the processes of nature, without using terms which imply reason and design. How can this difficulty be overcome ?

The mind, as axiomatically proved, has been developed from matter, and is matter. In its process of evolution from the atoms, it passed through the various stages in which the things in nature are still found. Now, when the atoms finally become mental they still retain impressions of their former states— that is, they still have an affinity for their former conditions, and with pleasure cherish their memory. When, therefore, the mind recognizes in things a likeness to itself—a reason, an intelligence—it is simply the unconscious remembrance of its former states. Everywhere the mind recognizes in nature old friends. It finds so much to correspond with its ideas, because it is nothing but matter, and in the matter outside of itself it sees forms like its own former self. The evidences of intelligence and design are therefore not a proof that there are intelligence and design in nature, just as there are in our minds, but that our minds are material like the things outside, and that these minds have passed through the forms of matter which are now recognized as affinities. In this original demonstration an important point is made for materialism.

There is therefore no design in nature. Even if there were, we could not recognize it, while the evidences against it are overwhelming. If a mind had impressed itself on nature we could not possibly know it; but that no mind has left its impress is so clear that one can shut his eyes and "see it feelingly."

The grand results achieved in this chapter will be better appreciated when it is remembered that the greatest minds could not banish design as we have done. Even the free-thinking Goethe failed to rid his mind of the idea of purpose in nature. At times his language is rather pantheistic; but his very pantheism arises from the universality of mind. "Nature has thought and is perpetually meditating," is one of his expressions.   He also said : " In contemplating the structure of the universe we cannot resist the notion that an idea lies at the basis of the whole." As an apology for the poet it may, however, be said that his mind was too full of reason and intellectual aspiration to rise to a conception of nature as thought-less and irrational.

There is no design—let it be repeated till all are convinced.   In man there is, of course, design.   He can act according to an intelligent plan ; he can give life a definite aim, and bend everything to its attain-ment.   Poor fool ! he is so full of design that it runs over into nature, and then he imagines that he dis-covers it there.   Man has design—so much of it, in fact, that he cannot think at all without discerning it around him.   But man, with all his design, is purely a product of nature ; therefore there is no design in nature.

CHAPTER VII.

MAN.

"What a piece of work is a man! How noble in reason! how infinite in faculty, in form, and moving, how express and admirable! in action, how like an angel! in apprehension, how like a god! the beauty of the world! the paragon of animals!"—HAMLET.

In reading Mr. Darwin's "Descent of Man" I have been struck with the facility with which humanity can be evolved from monkeys. If the anthropoid apes had only known that the process is so easy and natural, all of them would long ago have developed into men. If all that the book assumes is true, and if things really occurred as the author "believes," "suspects," and "thinks," and "regards probable," then the matter is settled. The scientific principle of probabilism luxuriates, and the logic built on it is overwhelming. The following is equal to anything in my own book : "So remarkable an instinct as the placing sentinels to warn the community of danger can hardly have been the indirect result of any other faculty ; it must, therefore, have been directly acquired."* The conclusion of the work is : "We thus learn that man is descended from a hairy quadruped, furnished with a tail and pointed ears, probably arboreal in its habits, and an inhabitant of the Old World."† A few pages

---

* XI. 82.   † II. 389.

further, he says : " The main conclusion arrived at in this work—namely, that man is descended from some lowly-organized form, will, I regret to think, be highly distasteful to many. But there can hardly be a doubt that we are descended from barbarians."* If there " can hardly be a doubt that we are descended from barbarians," then it is demonstrated that we are " descended from a hairy quadruped, furnished with a tail and pointed ears." The converse is also true : if we are the offspring of quadrupeds, there is hardly a doubt that we descended from barbarians. Generous as the author is with his assumptions, it is evident that many others might have been made which are still more probable ; and he who has talent to supply them will add much strength to the already invincible argument. But in spite of the marked skill displayed in adapting the logic to the popular taste, it is the authority of the author which gives the reasoning its weight.

I regard the origin of man as so firmly established that only the uninitiated can question the fact that he sprang from a lower form of animals. If man did not spring from the monkey, I cannot imagine how the arguments which prove it can be explained.

In getting the ape to father man we must heed a few important laws. Natural selection must be used freely. It is true that in the book mentioned its author says, in speaking of the earlier editions of his " Origin of Species" : " I probably attributed too much to the action of natural selection or the survival of the fittest."† Probably. Still, I think that we materialists may safely continue to shove much upon

_____

* II. 404.   † I. 152.

natural selection and attribute powers to it as liberally
as those do who have not yet learned that their master
modified his views. It is well known that species
readily pass over into each other, and that genera do
the same. Some supposed species have been proved
to be no species ; therefore there are no fixed species.
Since species and genera spontaneously transmute,
there is no telling what transformations are possible.
The law of transmutation is of important application
to man, who belongs to the ape family. Whatever is
peculiar to him we easily trace back to some animal,
and thus we prove that it is not peculiar. Thus intelligence is found throughout the whole animal creation ;
and to evolve man intellectually we need but suppose
that he is the same as a brute, and has had the proper environment and sufficient time to develop animal germs.

All this may be regarded as self-evident or as
demonstrated. Nevertheless, I always had great difficulty with reason while viewing it as the highest
faculty—the faculty for ideas and ideals, such as truth,
beauty, and goodness. Plato and Kant had perverted
my mind. From the latter I had learned that the ideas
of God, freedom, immortality are products of the
reason. But the difficulty vanishes altogether if we
still regard reason as the highest attribute of man, and
at the same time make it simply the discursive faculty,
or that which reasons. " Of all the faculties of the
human mind, it will, I presume, be admitted that
reason stands at the summit. Few persons any longer
dispute that animals possess some power of reasoning."* Mr. Darwin set me right. The sound of

---

* "Descent of Man," I. 46.

words determines their sense. The reason *reasons*, of course. This reasoning, then, is man's glory, and this is the summit on which he stands with other animals.

After reason had been properly levelled, I was still troubled with self-consciousness, abstraction, and general ideas ; but Mr. Darwin again got me right. The section on " Self-consciousness, Individuality, Abstraction, General Ideas, etc.,"* occupies about a page, and is introduced with these words : " It would be useless to attempt discussing these high faculties, which, according to several recent writers, make the sole and complete distinction between man and the brutes, for hardly two authors agree in their definitions." Strange that this had never before struck me ! This original way of disposing of the subject relieves the philosopher of all embarrassment. There is not the slightest doubt that if men agreed as to what self-consciousness, abstraction, and general ideas are they could easily be discovered in animals, or at least something from which sufficient time might have developed or transmuted them. If only morality and religion could also be disposed of with a single remark until it is agreed what they are, it would be still more easy to evolve man from the brute. But somehow they are unwilling to wait ; therefore the germs from which they grew must be found in other animals—a trifling matter, as the following chapters will show. In developing morals and religion the dog is very useful, some of the necessary germs being found in him to better advantage than in the ape. It is a general law that every human peculiarity is an animal development

---

* I. 62.

—a law significant for the sake of its consequences. Frequently the human germs in animals are but slightly developed, and instead of evolving manward they seem to have become stationary. Indeed, as the occasion requires we regard the germs as either stationary or evolvable, knowing perfectly in either case of what they are capable.

It would be stupid to object to this adaptability of the germs, since they belong to the unknowable from which the knowable is evolved. There must be variety in nature, and by its recognition science gains vivacity. When the origin of species is to be explained, let the species be transmutable, so variable, in fact, that the one fluently passes into another ; but when the fact that species are rigid is to be explained, then let the species be regarded as having attained permanence. The shrewd philosopher knows just when to use the opposite characteristics of species.

Laws unchangeable ? Only the obsolete ones of the Medes and Persians ; modern laws are for use, and have all the freedom, variety, and adaptability of life. If a child has a quality in a greater degree than the parent, the law of heredity is one of progress ; if in a less degree, then that same law works differently. If the child has anything which the parent has not, then it is a law of heredity that the child may have an endowment which the parent lacked ; but if the child fails to have a characteristic of the parent, then it is a law of heredity that children may lack what parents possessed. This admirable law, therefore, explains the appearance and disappearance, the increase and decrease of characteristics ; and if anything cannot be explained by that law it has not yet been discovered. Sometimes qualities are directly inherited ; sometimes a generation or two, or a thousand or more, may be skipped ; but all is wrought by the same law. Whatever similarity is found between parent and child is explained by the law of heredity ; and whatever dissimilarity is discovered is also a law of heredity. In the slow days of science a fact was only a fact ; now we can transmute every fact into a law.*

If man has properties to which an analogy can be discovered, or imagined, in the ape, it is a proof that he sprang from the ape ; those human qualities which can neither be found nor imagined in the ape prove that they have been evolved since he ceased to be a monkey ; and those characteristics of the ape which are not in man prove that the whole ape has not become human. A scientific adjuster of principles can thus discover man in the ape, and nothing but the ape in man. If we must have an unvarying law of universal application, here it is : all that is essential to man is that wherein he agrees with the ape ; that wherein he differs from his progenitor is unessential and purely accidental. With this law as our guide we explain the size and quality of man's brain, the teeth, extremities,

---

* In his "Reign of Law" the Duke of Argyll says of law : "But generally it is expressed in language vague and hollow, covering inaccurate conceptions, and confounding under common forms of expression ideas which are essentially distinct. The mere ticketing and orderly assortment. of external facts is constantly spoken of as if it were in the nature of an explanation, and as if no higher truth in respect to natural phenomena were to be attained or desired." The duke must have read some of my favorite authors. The general looseness in philosophy and science adds to their popularity. Is it not better to make the mere ticketing of facts our laws than to have no laws at all ?

and other physical peculiarities, as well as language, reason, self-consciousness, conscience, and religion.

Reason has already been disposed of ; other things can be settled by referring to Mr. Darwin or the authors whom he accepts as authorities. Difficulties vanish so quickly that we wonder how they ever came to be difficulties. Language has foolishly been supposed to be an obstacle to the evolution of the ape into man. But speech is simply the product of man's superior intellect, while his superior intellect can be explained as the product of his language. It may have occurred some other way, and likely did. The celebrated linguist, Lazarus Geiger, taught that reason did not create language, but that language created reason. Every part of speech preceded and occasioned the corresponding rational element. Thus language is originally not an expression of thought, but reason is the product of language. Professor Max Müller and others have also exercised their gifts in accounting for the origin of speech. But without stopping to consider the Ding-dong, or Bow-wow, and other theories, we hasten to Mr. Darwin's view of the origin of articulate language. He thinks " that primeval man, or rather some early progenitor of man, probably used his voice largely, as does one of the Gibbon apes at the present day, in producing true musical cadences—that is, in singing ; we may conclude from a widely-spread analogy that this power would have been especially exerted during the courtship of the sexes, serving to express various emotions, as love, jealousy, triumph, and serving as a challenge to their rivals. The imitation by articulate sounds of musical cries might have given rise to words expressive of various complex

emotions.   .   .   .   As monkeys certainly understand
much that is said to them by man, and as in a state
of nature they utter signal-cries of danger to their
fellows, it does not appear altogether incredible that
some unusually wise ape-like animal should have
thought of imitating the growl of a beast of prey, so
as to indicate to his fellow-monkeys the nature of the
expected danger.   And this would have been a first
step in the formation of a language."* In their
courtship the monkeys may have used some of "the
siren notes of a poetical natural science," of which Professor Virchow speaks.   The courtship origin of language receives further confirmation from cats, which
under similar circumstances also cultivate their vocal
organs.   Since no one has given the facts proving that
language did not originate in this affectionate manner,
we are justified in saying with Mr. Darwin that the
faculty of articulate speech offers no " insuperable objection to the belief that man has been developed from
some lower form."   And if language by itself offers
no *insuperable* objection to this *belief*, and if the same
can be said of many other faculties of man, would it
not be better to lump the not-insuperable objections
and just regard it as *demonstrated* that man is the result of ape-culture ?

We shall make better progress by laying aside com-
parative psychology, and, in fact, all psychology.
" Above all, let us stick to that which can be measured
and weighed ;" and I propose an improvement on
Mr. Vogt's dictum by adding—and let it be made the
standard of all that cannot be measured and weighed.

* I. 56.

We shall then do consciously what has so generally been followed as an unconscious law. Why take into account what has neither ounces nor inches, the sole standards of reality? If such objects obtrude themselves on the attention, abundant precedent can be found for disposing of them with some frivolous remark.

Professor Huxley* thinks he has shown that physically there are greater differences between the higher and the lower apes than between man and the higher apes—that is, the quantitative differences are greater, for of the qualitative ones science knows nothing. Carl Vogt finds in idiots a striking illustration that man must be a descendant of the ape. In those who are born idiots the development of the brain, especially the front part, was checked during the period of gestation; hence the idiocy. Seeing in these unfortunate beings a marked similarity to apes, he comes to this conclusion: "If, however, it is possible for man to be brought nearer the ape by checking his formation and development, then the law of development must be the same for both, and we cannot question the possibility that, just as man can sink to the level of the ape by checking his development, so the ape, by continuing his development, can come nearer man." The only thing here assumed is that the ape *can* continue this development in the manner required—a necessary assumption, since on it the whole argument rests. Undoubtedly he could if reasonably encouraged. In a good cause it is perfectly proper to judge a normal by an abnormal state, provided other illustrations cannot be found.

* " Man's Place in Nature."

If we suppose the brain of the ape the same in *kind* as that of man, and also susceptible of an equal degree of development ; and if we suppose that the intellect is *purely* a product of the brain, I do not see why the human intellect cannot be developed from the simian. That there are idiots, but no humanized apes, of course cannot affect those whose hypotheses are superior to facts.

Highly as I prize the demonstrations of Professors Huxley and Vogt, I prefer to go a little deeper, because the results will be more satisfactory. The former considers only the physical structure of man, and the latter takes him at the period of gestation, when the supposed ape-stage is reached. I propose to go back to the germ. Here all the required similarity between man and the ape is found. Comparing the egg from which the one springs with that of the other, no essential difference is seen ; therefore both are alike. This demonstrates the fact that the only difference between man and ape is the result of development. And by comparing the eggs of some other animals no differences are discernible ; this proves that man is the same as the lower animals—another illustration of the advantage of going to the bottom of things. A philosophic mind prefers the germ to the matured product. In the product it is limited to that which *is ;* in the germ the fancy is limited only by itself. That modern scientist is to be pitied who cannot find in the germ what inductive science fails to discover in the most perfectly developed plant or animal.*

---

* Instead of first reducing all that is human to the level of the brute, and then finding its germs in the lower animals, we might

After thus demonstrating that man ascended from the apes, we can now trace the paternity more definitely. Evidently man descended from that monkey which is most like man, or which was most like him when he was evolved. A modern scientist has declared that man, especially the negro, stretches out his hand to the highest apes, not quite reaching them. May not this be explained by the fact that man's arm has been considerably shortened since he became human? If his arms and other parts did not differ so much from the ape he might not only reach the monkey, but also walk with him arm in arm as his brother and intellectual peer.

But from which one? The question were easily answered if the missing link, for which I myself have diligently and hopefully sought, could be found. After long and vain search I concluded that in hunting that link I made a fool of myself. While it is missing it cannot be found ; if it were found it would not be *missing ;* therefore there is no missing link. But in spite of this and all other gaps, which can be filled without difficulty, I hold to man's descent from the apes, just as Professor Vogt does, with him looking hopefully and confidently into the future for those

---

begin with the animals, and reason up to man. The animal germs will no doubt willingly evolve into humanity. Whatever is still found in man which cannot be thus explained may be regarded as somehow the transmutation of something or other in the brute.

I beg pardon for occasionally letting the word *brute* slip out. Since man has been proved to be nothing but an animal he has become peculiarly sensitive about calling brutes brutes. Unless I forget myself, I shall hereafter call the brutes animals, and some of them anthropoid animals.

discoveries which are still needed to establish the fact which I have demonstrated.

It has been suspected that there must have been a great many gradations between the ape and man, so that the process of evolution was gradual. This may have been the case ; but after the first human pair had been successfully modelled, the law of the survival of the fittest saved them, but destroyed the gradations. It is a general law that intermediates between the various species are only necessary in order to produce one pair of a fixed species ; becoming useless after that, they disappear, in order not to confuse the characteristic marks of the species. For the same reason the inter-mediates have vanished even from the geologic strata. That they existed is evident, for how else could there have been the proper transmutation of one species into another ?

The disappearance of intermediates may also be ac-counted for by wiping out all distinction between man and monkey. In that case they never existed. Or it may be that the passage from ape to man was a sudden leap—a miraculous, mythological transformation, which startled both the father and his son. The "unusually wise ape-like animal" of Mr. Darwin, which to him "does not appear altogether incredible" to have aided in forming language, might be utilized. Why could not the simian courtship result in men as well as lan-guage ? In that case the monkey leaped over the in-termediates into men.

It has been suspected that if monkeys once became men they ought still to go through the same process of evolution. And who knows that this is not the case ? Perhaps the new tribes discovered from time to time in

Africa originated in that way. The fact that they had never before been observed in the unexplored wilds of that continent is presumptive evidence that they have recently emerged from apes. Some of them suggest an intimate relation to their ancestors by various physical and mental characteristics. I myself have seen a negro lad scratch his head precisely as a monkey does. This remarkable physical phenomena led me to inquire into the psychical element lying at its basis ; and on investigation I found to my astonishment that their motives were exactly the same. This surprising physical and psychical coincidence led me to prosecute my researches still more deeply in the same direction. In both cases I procured the final causes of the scratching, and examined them under the microscope. My suspicions were confirmed ; the likeness was too striking to be accidental. The spectrum analysis also revealed exactly the same lines, and by this unfailing test I demonstrated the relationship of the two Africans (I mean the lad and the monkey, not the final causes).

This original proof of the origin of man is my own, but equally convincing ones may be found in the works of Mr. Darwin and Professor Vogt. I find in fact that their original researches are strikingly confirmatory of mine. When the former says,* " Social animals perform many little services for each other : horses nibble, and cows lick each other, on any spot which itches ; monkeys search for each other's external parasites," it can be comprehended without difficulty how the nibble and the lick, as well as the itch, could be developed into humanity. " Monkeys

* I. 74–5.

search for each other's *external* parasites !"   Who does
not see in this touching scene the affectionate mother
and her darling child !   Whether the apes also search
for each other's *internal* parasites with vermifuge my
authorities fail to state.

Since it has been so clearly demonstrated that man
can be evolved from the ape, nothing now remains but
to do it.   Why, amid the luxuriant culture of the age,
not have some *human* culture—I mean the culture of
apes into men ?   What has been done in the past can
be done again, especially if we use our chemical and
physical appliances half as skilfully as our logic.
After demonstrating men into monkeys, and then
monkeys into men, I have wondered why our anthropological societies have no separate section for evolving men from apes.   Keeping the animals in zoological gardens has not developed any striking human
qualities ; and the efforts at private training and school-
ing have been rather unsatisfactory.   But if a family,
or two, of each variety of apes were procured and put
into an institution specially prepared for them, under
skilful breeders and wise teachers, I cannot see why
ape-culture should not result in human culture.   The
progress annually made by each family might be recorded and discussed by the Simian Section of the
Anthropological Society.   By thus introducing new
elements into humanity the stock might be rejuve-
nated and improved.   But I am well aware that there
are serious objections to this kind of evolution, so I
doubt whether it will ever be tried.   The trial might
make the impression that the theory of man's descent
is in doubt and needs confirmation from facts.   Such
an experimental test might also prove injurious to

science by promoting the inductive instead of the deductive method, and by again substituting facts for hypotheses. Then, too, in those districts where the experiment would likely be tried there would be danger of overproduction if the culture succeeded ; especially would there be a surplus of the kind of persons likely to be produced by the experiment.

But which ape ? Pious reverence for one's ancestors, and an earnest desire to do them full justice in our hearts and memories, naturally encourage profound investigations with a filial spirit. The human culture suggested would no doubt decide whether it was gibbon, mandrill, orang, gorilla, or chimpanzee. Perhaps they crossed and got mixed, so that man is a mongrel. If he is a hybrid, man is probably an orphan, or else his ancestors have become various. There are strong reasons for believing that he is the product of a variety of combinations, all of which have long ago ceased to exist ; then man searches in vain for his forefathers. Mr. Darwin's " ape-like animal" meets all the required conditions. Since no one knows anything about it, we can invest it with the required attributes without fear of contradiction. Nor is there any serious objection to Mr. Vogt's former view, that the Americans sprang from an American, the Africans from an African, and the Asiatics from an Asiatic ape. The theory of man's simian origin is blessed with numerous other possibilities equally reliable and all confirmatory of its truth.

It may seem childish, but ever since reading Darwin and the Darwinians, especially the luxuriant ones on the continent, I feel an irresistibly intense desire to press tenderly and reverently the hand of every monkey I meet, under the conviction that we had a common ancestor and that the difference between us is owing to environment, or something else. A feeling of native pride and gratitude overcomes me when I remember whence I sprang and what I have become. There is really much more glory in developing a man from a monkey than from a human egg or embryo, for this egg has the peculiar qualities which must, under proper circumstances, develop into man and form all his peculiar characteristics. Indeed, it cannot help itself—it need but unfold, and man is its direct and natural product. But to evolve him from the ape, a brute with less brains and less sense and less cunning and less skill than some animals which have not yet become anthropoid ; to develop him into Plato, Kant, and final scientists, with absolutely no further additions than such as naturally accrue in the process of evolution—this is an achievement inconceivably glorious. It may be that the fathers have degenerated as much as their children have progressed ; at any rate the descent is an ascent. Man is the aristocrat of his family, " the paragon of animals."

I am somewhat slower than some other scientists in evolving man from the ape, realizing that the dignity of the subject is worthy of deliberation. Inordinate haste might take the fatal step from the sublime to the ridiculous, which I zealously strive to avoid. It requires time to develop the grin of the monkey into the gravity of man.

Another thing makes the thoughtful man pause : modern scientists have developed us from monkeys in so many ways that it is exceedingly difficult for us to

make a choice.* The nature of man's origin has frequently been settled finally, but has always been unsettled again. Philosophers have failed to agree on
the nature of that which is to be taken for granted—a
subject on which all can afford to be generous. But
even where there is agreement in assumptions there
are conflicts in the conclusions, so that in the manifold-
ness of man's descent no point is settled except that he
sprang from an ape, or from various apes, or from
some ancestor of the apes, or from some other now extinct animals, or in some other way. The most definite
result of the whole discussion of the subject is therefore that the nature of man's origin is not definitely
settled. But this does not interfere with the definite
opinions of individuals. I have long ago settled the
problem "of the origin of man out of chaos, by means
of the play of the atoms determined mathematically
from eternity to eternity." The atoms worked up to
man through the inferior animals, especially through
the apes, or some now extinct and unknown, but variously imagined ancestor.

I rejoice that Mr. Vogt changed his view that man
sprang from an American, an African, and an Asiatic
ape. What is the use of tying us to monkeys with a
threefold cord when one is sufficient? His later
opinion is that man did not spring from the apes at
all, but from their ancestors. These reared two
families—one of apes, another of men. Whether it
was blood, or training, or environment which made
the difference is immaterial. Apes are therefore our

* The pleasing variety in the accounts of man's origin may be
seen in Wigand's "Darwinismus," III.

brothers, sisters, and cousins, instead of fathers and mothers. Since absolutely nothing can be determined respecting these ancestors, this theory (which he may have changed again by this time) also has the advantage of freedom from the restraint of facts. Professor Haeckel and Mr. Darwin regard the father of the anthropoid apes as also the parent of the human family ; therefore the ancestor of man no longer exists. Some scientists, especially those who are sticklers for facts and have not been properly disciplined in modern logic, reject the ape theory altogether ; but until another relative is found who can claim a nearer kinship with man, the preponderance of evidence and affection is in favor of the simia.

Those who have demonstrated that the ape is the lost ancestor have their peculiar notions as to *what* and *where* and *how* he was. The marked differences in their conclusions of course depend on the peculiar facts which each one examined. Darwin put the parents in Africa, Wagner in Europe, Spiller in the polar regions and high mountains, Haeckel in Southern Asia or in Lemuria, a sunken continent south of Asia, and of late he has kindly concluded to leave the question open. Australia has some decided advantages : I have seen an Australian climb a tree like a monkey —a very suggestive fact ! The islands of the sea also afford numerous unused possibilities, and he who seeks the reputation of originality can take any one of them and furnish it as the home of our ancestors. The subject is worthy of scientific consideration, since the real spot may not yet have been discovered.

Mr. Darwin viewed our ancestor as hairy, though this involved him in some difficulty and more poetry in

getting man unhaired.* Natural selection will not
account for the unhairing process ; it was therefore
done by sexual selection. " We know that the faces
of several species of monkeys and large surfaces at the
posterior end of the body in other species have been
denuded of hair ; and this we may safely attribute to
sexual selection, for these surfaces are not only vividly
colored, but sometimes, as with the male mandrill and
female rhesus, much more vividly in the one sex than
in the other." These bright colors were admired by
our ancestors, and thus we get a glimpse of the germ
which developed into the taste of a Raphael. Natural
and sexual selection came in conflict ; but this conflict
is explained by showing that it is common. " Nor is
it surprising that a character in a slight degree injurious
should have been thus acquired ; for we know that
this is the case with the plumes of some birds and
with the horns of some stags."

We may imagine various ways in which the unhairing began. This is Mr. Darwin's explanation : " The
females of certain anthropoid apes, as stated in a
former chapter, are somewhat less hairy on the under
surface than are the males ; and here we have what
might have afforded a commencement for the process
of denudation." Certainly it " might have ;" and
there is no doubt that the process seized this opportunity.

Mr. Wallace viewed the ancestor naked. Indeed,
the shaggy question, like some others, is still an open
one. I do not, however, regard the conflicting views
of Darwin and Wallace respecting the clothing as a

---

* II. 375.

serious obstacle in the way of the evolution. Although the subject is extremely interesting, it really makes little difference whether the ancestor was hairy, or woolly, or naked, if only he was truly the ancestor. If he lived at the poles, he was hairy, otherwise he would have caught cold ; if at the equator, he was naked, for with a fur coat the heat would have been uncomfortable ; if between the two, he was partly naked, partly hairy. If he was naked in equatorial regions the burning sun would scorch blisters on a tender skin ; his hide may therefore have resembled that of a rhinoceros. The contradictory views can thus be harmonized. Let us have peace.

The tail can hardly be regarded one of the unsettled points, since the chimpanzee, gibbon, orang, and gorilla have none ; and even if they had, a rudimentary one might be found in man. Mr. Darwin explicitly states that the ancestor was " furnished with a tail and pointed ears." These ears are not always rudimentary in man.

By adding some of my own embellishments, I have concluded to regard Mr. Haeckel's view of the sunken continent as the ancestral home as demonstrated. The advantages of the theory give its discovery the unmistakable stamp of genius. It accounts for the disappearance of the ancestors, and the intermediates, from the face of the earth as well as from the geologic strata, and all questions respecting them can be laid to rest till the sunken continent is explored ; it makes the missing link a sunken one, and thus gives the reason why it is missing ; it saves the trouble of looking for immediate kindred outside of the human family, for they may have been drowned when the continent

sank ; it absolves us from describing minutely what
the ancestors were, and through what stages man
passed as he grew up after his ancestor left him to
shift for himself, since every trace and record was
lost ; it explains the early accounts and traditions of a
deluge, which was nothing but the sinking of this
continent, from which men escaped in canoes, or by
swimming, to America, Asia, and Africa ; and the
theory has still other advantages. Here the genesis
and exodus of humanity occurred, and here prehistoric
man wrote the first page of human history. True, its
author has abandoned this theory ; but that should not
excite any prejudice against it, for it is fully as rational
as others to which he tenaciously clings. Occasionally
there is more truth without than within a man's faith.

Nothing is known of this continent except that it *is*
sunken and *was* the home of our ancestors and of our
infant race ; but this is enough ; other data we can
supply. The climate was mild, and so the first men
and women, needing no clothing, could be born naked.
Nature kindly furnished food in abundance, thus giving the infant race an opportunity to devote itself un-
reservedly to the much-needed intellectual and moral
culture, to the formation of language, and to the production of literature and the development of political
institutions. All that is attributed to primitive man
and his forefathers which occurred nowhere else took
place here. It was, consequently, a lively continent.
Respecting the lost history something may be learned
by watching the human expression of the emotions,
since men then felt and looked, laughed and cried,
just as they do now. Some of the expressions are explained by the rule of similarity ; others by that of

difference ; others still by that of contrariety ; others
by a mixture of any two or all three. There is no
difficulty in interpreting any expression after it has
been decided what it shall mean ; and in every instance the emotion and its expression may be traced,
by lineal descent, to the submerged continent and the
inferior animals.

This paradise at least is not mythological. The
conditions being specially favorable, the atoms here
first succeeded in creating life, and here, too, occurred
the great transmutations of species, as well as the birth
of man ; it was the cradle of that heterogeneity now
everywhere apparent. When the species still existing
had been evolved, the continent sank, and the animals
which were not drowned, or made aquatic, swam to the
neighboring continents. Since that time the transmutations have continued only to a limited extent.

During the transmutation era the species passed
vigorously into each other ; and those which had been
successfully transmuted perished. During the process
of transmutation the degrees were distinctly marked,
so that every stage of the progress could easily be
traced. The reversions were also very numerous, and
it was common for the species already finished to
revert, by regular gradations, to their originals. Animated nature was quite checkered by this progress
and regress. All these processes are distinctly marked
in the geologic strata of that continent, though we are
unfortunately deprived of the privilege of examining
them. Indeed, that geology proves that the inter-
mediate were more numerous than the fixed types ;
therefore it is called the transmutation era.

The age of this era can be determined by geologic

data. In this way we learn approximately the age of the fixed species, of man, and of the sinking of the continent. Sceptics point to ancient descriptions and representations of animals to prove that they were the same then as now ; to the mummies of Egypt ; to the seed thousands of years old, which, if sown now, produces the same kind of grain as that of the present day ; Agassiz found the corals on the coast of Florida and in the Pacific Ocean, estimated to be twenty or thirty thousand years old, the same as those now in the process of formation ; and the records of geology, as well as the present stability of species, are also used against the established truth of the transmutation of species. But all these arguments amount to nothing, since the transmutations occurred before the preserved records were made, and then the continent went under ! The existing records down to the tertiary period hardly favor the activity of transmutation, for they prove the stability of different species with a tenacity amounting to obstinacy. Transmutation must therefore have spent its zeal and accomplished its main work before the deposits of the tertiary period. This gives us a safe and definite starting-point for reckoning time. Man was evolved, the species were transmuted, the continent sank before or at the beginning of the tertiary age. The exact year might be found by mathematicians, but it is hardly worth while, since a few millions of years more or less are of no account in geology.

When the animals and incipient men reached the still existing continents, they first settled along the shores, acclimated themselves, studied their environment, and adapted themselves to it, thus still undergoing slight transformations. Those failing to adapt themselves either perished or emigrated inland until they found a congenial clime and surroundings. Those which succeeded best in adapting themselves to circumstances were naturally selected for the survival of the fittest ; they lived, reared families, and transmitted the fittest qualities. At that time the survival of the fittest was no new discovery, and created no surprise ; for in their *naïve*, uncultivated state those natural men imagined that it was self-evident that those fit to live should outlive those which were unfit, and that the fittest should survive just because they were fittest.

After dovetailing together as best I could the various opinions on man's origin, I revolved in my mind some of the choice morsels of materialism which are more or less established by this chapter. One materialist declares that there is no essential difference between instinct and reason ;* another says : " Not a single intellectual capacity belongs to man alone ;" † another : " The ideal is nothing but the material as transformed in the human brain ;" ‡ another : " Materiality is the sole peculiarity of all reality ; and all that seems to us to be ideal, therefore also spirit and soul, is only the motion of the molecules, which is a property of matter ;" and he holds that " conscious thought is the sole product of the molecular motion of the atoms of the brain ;" § and another teaches that " the human body is a modified animal form ; the human soul is an animal soul intensified." ‖ These

---

* Krahmer. † Büchner. ‡ Marx.
§ Engels. ‖ Burmeister.

sound materialistic dogmas confirm the conclusions of
this chapter, and I was pondering the completeness of
my demonstrations when the " Proceedings of the German Anthropological Society at Frankfurt, 1882," fell
into my hands. As these Germans have long ago laid
aside all religious prejudices, I eagerly looked for con-
firmations of my views, but soon found it best to say
as little as possible about those Proceedings. A few
illustrations will make this evident. The President of
the Society, Professor Lucæ, said of Darwin's " Origin
of Species," that it had led some investigators in a
direction the opposite of the inductive method " because they sought their proofs *a priori.*" Certainly ;
that is our glory, and we propose to stick to that
method. Where else can we get them ? Speaking of
the efforts of this tendency to prove that man is a descendant of the ape, he says : " This tendency began
with the appearance of the gorilla, reached its scientific culmination in Darwin's ' Origin of Species,' exploded as brilliant fireworks in Haeckel's ' History of
Creation,' and ended sadly with Darwin's ' Descent of
Man.' " With profound sorrow I read that the skull
of the Neanderthal is now declared not to prove anything respecting man's relation to apes, while from
that found in the Engis Cave the President draws the
conclusion " that man in that primitive age had the
same formation of skull as in our day." If even
these skulls fail us, what are human confidence and
hope worth ? There was much more of the same sort.
Professor Huxley's important conclusion that the
difference between man and the chimpanzee, or gorilla,
is less than that between the gorilla and the other
apes, is declared to have been completely refuted.

The President said : " While Mr. Aeby and I successfully opposed Mr. H., by means of proofs from the
bones of many apes, that thorough anatomist and
physiologist, Mr. Bischoff, proved, step by step, the
untenableness of Mr. H.'s claim, by extensive exami-
nations of the hand and foot of nearly all known apes,
as well as by a careful examination of the brain ; and
Professor Brühl refuted his claim as far as the chimpanzee is concerned, and Mr. C. Langer respecting
the orang." But what business had they to meddle
with the matter after Professor Huxley had settled it
finally ? What becomes of Mr. Darwin's " Descent
of Man," which assumes that " in the opinion of
most competent judges" the professor had proved his
point, if, now, it is not established ?

Mr. Darwin's ancestor of man was rudely pronounced a myth, and this declaration is based on the
examination of skulls of apes from different countries !
It was openly stated that the cohorts of Darwinian
apostles, who in all lands proclaim to the laity " the
revealed secrets of creation," are losing caste, while
inductive scientists are gaining ground ; and it seems
that even the masses have been nauseated by the revelations of inspired Darwinians !

Mortified and disgusted by these statements of the
President, I turned for consolation to Professor Virchow, whose address was in commemoration of Mr.
Darwin and his great services to science. But I cannot now remember that it gave me any particular
comfort or encouragement. Speaking of the empirical
basis on which the society rests, he asserted that
" even when the waves of Darwinism rose highest,
the German Anthropological Society did not lose its

senses." Does the learned professor mean to insinuate that any persons did? He gives as the reason why the society kept its senses the fact that it had experienced investigators, "and not such as were mere beginners." Is this, too, an insinuation?

With a marked lack of delicacy, the Berlin scholar says of those who have zealously speculated the ape into man : " They have taken possession of the ape, and have performed with him extensive and ludicrous dances." Now if we Darwinians are pleased to dance with apes for the sake of familiarizing ourselves with their antics and studying their anthropoid qualities, need any one poke fun at us for our devotion to science? I may have felt too deeply chagrined at finding so serious a matter treated with levity ; but I had just finished my chapter on man's origin when the address fell into my hands.

Speaking of the transition from animals to man, Professor Virchow strangely says that none of the evidences of this transition have been produced, though they ought to exist if man was thus evolved ! But this objection has been anticipated by putting the transition on the sunken continent, and all can now see the wisdom of there permitting the ape to evolve himself. The professor adds : " Never has any one discovered a being which was just becoming man, or, better still, a pre-man (Vormensch) ; he was always found already finished. All that we now know, even the oldest discoveries which have been made, were already complete men. The *Proanthropos* must still be sought ; and he who wants to find him will probably have to go a great way." Certainly ; to the sunken continent.

There is something discouraging in these Proceedings, which show that proof on proof was produced, from skulls and other things, that repeatedly when men have exclaimed in finding remains of man, " c'est un type simien !" they were found to be nothing but human.   That very address which commemorated Mr. Darwin's great services declares that he gave no proofs of man's descent from the lower animals.   An astounding assertion !   But enough has been said to indicate that to us this society is of no earthly significance.   It has too many demonstrators and not enough creators.

CHAPTER VIII.

" Only this I know, if what thou namest Happiness be our true
aim, then are we all astray.   With Stupidity and sound Digestion
man may front much.   But what in these dull, unimaginative
days are the terrors of conscience to the diseases of the liver !
Not on morality, but on cookery, let us build our stronghold ;
there brandishing our frying-pan, as censer, let us offer sweet in-
cense to the Devil, and live at ease on the fat things *he* has provided for his Elect !"—CARLYLE.

AFTER the demonstration that man is purely an
evolution of matter through apes, it is a necessary
truth that all he possesses must also be the product of
this evolution.   There is profound wisdom in first
proving that man was thus evolved, and then drawing
the necessary inferences respecting morality and religion.   If we were obliged first to demonstrate that
these are animal endowments, humanly developed, it
might complicate and prejudice man's origin ; but
after his origin is settled there can be no doubt that
morality and religion are the blossom and fruit of
germs here profusely scattered, there sparsely sprinkled, through the whole animal creation.

There are notions of morality which offer insuperable difficulties to the view that they are developed
animal traits ; such conceptions must consequently be
false.   Since morals are a product of the animal developed through man, nothing belongs to morality
unless it is so evolved.

In materialistic morality nothing foreign is grafted
on matter ; it is as purely material as is the stone.
All that exists is the result of necessary law ; therefore morality is responsible neither for its existence
nor for its character.   One kind is just as necessary,
just as reliable, just as true, and just as right, as another.   But modern scientific morality, while also
purely natural, is of course the highest evolution of
ethical matter under the judicious direction of physical laws.

The atoms cannot at once leap into ethics ; but by
passing through various evolutions they finally attain
so lofty a development that they can rub out morality.
The atoms themselves cannot change ; we consequently evolve the universe by atomic friction.   By
rubbing together their outsides the atoms produce the
inorganic world ; by rubbing together their insides
they evolve the organic ; and by rubbing together
both their outsides and insides they create mental
phenomena.   Ordinary mental phenomena are the
product of an equilibrium between the external and
internal rubbing ; when the internal friction is more
violent than the external we have the genesis of
morality and religion.*

----

* Only those not familiar with the possibilities of atoms will
object to this explanation.   A materialist might swear that in this
way all his morals and religion are produced, and no one would
question his word or suspect him of perjury.   If anything is to
be explained, let the atoms move and twirl and dance and rub !
The ethical and the spiritual is in them, and can be churned out.

A friend suggests that certain popular philosophic works were
produced by the atoms when turned upside down.   This is probable ; but they must have continued their rubbing in that posture,
for they produce nothing except by friction.

Various affections of the mind depend on the swift-
ness of the atoms ; the degrees in these affections are
the result of quantity, so that the thought will be
active and the feeling intense in proportion to the
number of the atoms. Intensity may also be the product of rapidity of motion, but this is not confirmed
by observation. We cannot conceive how consciousness can result from a union of independent atoms ; it
is therefore better to create it some other way. When
one atom rubs against another and strikes hard, it
makes an impression on the other atom, arouses its
attention, makes revelations to it, and thus creates
consciousness. This is the general form of consciousness found in all animals. When an atom is in profound solitude, and so rubs itself as to turn its inside
out and its outside in, and then examines both sides
and also their relations to each other, self-consciousness is produced. (This is Fichte's Ich or Ego.)
When this self-consciousness compares itself, by means
of friction, with all the other atoms, it develops
itself into a world-consciousness, or a consciousness of
the world. Self-consciousness is the eye (or atom)
which sees itself ; a consciousness of the world is the
eye viewing the world ; and consciousness as a whole
is a mirror which sees itself as well as the objects
which it reflects.

When atoms rub externally first and then internally,
they produce sensations—the external penetrating the
internal, which is the essence of all sensation. When
they rub internally first and then externally, they
create the phenomena of the will, which is a process
from the inner to the outer. Between these two
processes lie all the phenomena of thought and emo-

tion. All thought being founded on sensation, it is the product of the external rubbing of the atoms, which works effects in the interior—thought being simply the product of working over internally the results of external friction. By heaping the effects of the several rubbings we get general ideas ; by pleasant rubbing, as when an itchy spot is scratched, we get the pleasurable emotions ; and by eliminating the rubbing, the atoms, and everything else, we get abstractions, or, rather, we imagine that we get them, for in reality we get nothing, all that is real having been abstracted.

While this psychology of the atoms was prepared for the purpose of throwing light on all their mental processes, the main thing which concerns us here is the evolution of morals and religion which, as demonstrated, are thrown off by the harder internal than external rubbing. That this is really the process is also evident from the fact that they are chiefly internal, being matters of the conscience and the heart, while their outward form is but a revelation of the inner state.

Conscience is the principal factor and supreme guide in morals. It is not peculiar to man, but is found in a rudimentary or germinal state in all animals. The germs of conscience in brutes would, if sufficiently developed, render their possessors as moral as some men are. In the dog, for instance, there are signs of fear, which can be made analogous to the moral sense in man. The wagging of the tail is a moving evidence of the approval of conscience, while remorse is expressed by a rigid depression of the same member. Traces of conscience have also been found

in monkeys ; when their consciences were aroused by
scolding they have shown signs of fear, an unmistakable evidence that they discerned between right and
wrong.   Monkeys have been known to extract thorns
from each other's hide " conscientiously," which is
highly significant !

The exact locality of conscience in brutes has not
received the scientific attention it deserves ; we cannot therefore determine just where it has been deposited by the friction.   It is probable that the moral
sense of monkeys is in their grimaces ; cats have it in
the paws, dogs in the nose.   Where it is located in
mules is not known, but it is aroused by tickling their
hind legs.   Indeed, with the right spirit, vestiges of
conscience can be found anywhere ; therefore morality
is only a scarecrow, which cannot frighten materialists
from a hearty recognition of their relation to the
brutes.

Mr. Darwin indeed says that man " alone can with
certainty be ranked as a moral being ;" but numerous
other remarks deprive this one of its edge.   Thus he
thinks it in a high degree probable " that any animal
whatever, endowed with well-marked social instincts,
would inevitably acquire a moral sense or conscience,
as soon as its intellectual powers had become as well
developed, or nearly as well developed, as in man." *
It may at least be said in favor of this view that all
social animals which have submitted to this development of their intellectual powers have acquired a
moral sense.   And it is well known that men are
always moral in proportion as they are social and intel-

* I. 71.

lectual. We of course take it for granted that every-body recognizes morality as simply a union of the social and intellectual elements !

Professor Vogt does not agree with Mr. Darwin that man "alone can with certainty be ranked as a moral being." With his wonderful gift of scientific interpretation he can no doubt find morality wherever he sees fit to exert his ingenuity. He says : "Look at a family of cats or bears, watch the conduct of the young, their training by the old, and then state whether there is not found there a picture of the human family, with all those manifestations of the notion of good and evil which any one can demand ! I admit that it is cat-morality or bear-morality which is here taught and instilled into the children, but nevertheless it is morality ; and the young cat which does not come at the call of the mother, the two-year-old bear which does not properly take care of its brothers and sisters, are growled at and receive a box on the ear, just as the dear human children do if they ignore the first conception of human and Christian morality—namely, filial obedience." *

Here we have a moral sense, moral training, and morality in animals. Truly a striking "picture of the human family" ! It is evident that if this thing is morality, then morality is found in brutes. This morality which is growled and beaten into juvenile cats and bears is exactly the same as that which is snarled and whipped into human children ; and it is never taught in any other way, and, in fact, cannot be. Conscience not found in brutes ? The morals

---

* Ueber den Menschen, I. 295.

"taught and instilled into the children" in this way
might, in fact, with propriety be called brutal rather
than human. Sweet memories must haunt the man
whose "first conception of human and Christian
morality" was communicated in this way, and he is a
fit subject to become the world's moral teacher and
guide.

Female apes "carry their young to the water-side
and there wash their faces, in spite of resistance and
cries." This important, ethical fact is quoted by Professor Huxley and Mr. Darwin, and is now ready to
go the rounds of the modern tread-mill of natural
philosophy. That the *mother*-apes wash their children
proves the domestic institutions of apes to be remark-
ably similar to those of the human family ; and that
the mother-apes wash the faces in spite of resistance
and cries, is a demonstration that their moral sense is
stronger than maternal affection. From the training
received it is probable that ape-morality differs somewhat from the cat and bear kind. Monkeys are early
taught that cleanliness is next to godliness—a lesson
which if learned by some of their keepers in zoological
gardens would improve the odor of their sanctity.

It has also been observed that an ape which had
once or twice been scolded for taking a piece of soap,
took it again (how suggestive of the moral traits of
some naughty children !) ; when quietly spoken to by
his master, the ape, observing that he had been caught
in the very act, returned the soap nearly in the same
place whence he had taken it. This is simply astounding, when we remember that many a precocious boy,
under similar circumstances, would have flatly refused
to return the soap, and might have become impudent

besides.   It is not surprising therefore that Mr. Huxley sees in this act (that of the monkey) an evidence
of "a certain conscience." I should say—of obedience, respect, reverence, homage, worship ; we have
here the religious faculty in a highly developed form.
The conscience of the monkey did not act until he saw
that he was discovered—which is always an essential
element, and a sure sign, of conscience.

There are men who have the morality of particular
brutes, as of dogs, or wolves, or hyenas ; and some
have none at all.   Such facts make it so clear that
there is nothing peculiar in the human morality
which is found in brutes, that nothing more need be
said on the subject.   The study of psychology, and
investigations respecting the freedom of the will only
serve to confuse the study of ethics ; they are properly omitted here, since we aim strictly at scientific
accuracy.

Having now reduced morality to the proper level
by eliminating all that is foreign to brutes, we are
prepared to search for the supreme good, that object
which is most worthy of the ambition of man and
other moral animals.   What, above all other things,
should be made the aim of life ?   The answer will
give the basis of all morality.   I answer unhesitatingly : for man and beast the *useful* and *agreeable*
is the supreme good.   This is the pole-star of ethics,
to which the needle of conscience always points.

Whatever is useful is right ; whatever is not useful
is wrong.   This is the essence of the materialistic
decalogue.   Whoever chooses the useful and the agreeable (the two being convertible terms) is always right.
If the atoms have evolved necessity into freedom, so

that a man has become responsible, he commits a crime if he chooses anything injurious, provided he knows that the ultimate result of the choice will be an injury ; but if the atoms have not evolved freedom, he will recognize no responsibility, and will see in crime only a mistake. The process of materialistic evolution is now advancing so rapidly that freedom will in every case be proved a necessity ; every choice will be shown to be unavoidable ; nothing but mechanical laws will be recognized as supreme ; crimes will be converted into errors of judgment, and remorse into regrets ; * that will be the dawn of the Millennium !

Materialistic morality, being purely utilitarian, promotes the useful to the utmost ; it is consequently the highest and most agreeable. There is a commonplace moral standpoint for Philistines, who claim that right is the highest principle and that it ought to be done for its own sake. This vulgar view holds that the universe is so constructed that right and truth and happiness will finally be completely harmonized, and that from right the greatest usefulness and happiness will flow as a necessary consequence. This principle

---

* Remorse is regret intensified, of course. Any regret, if heightened, becomes remorse, a striking confirmation of the theory of evolution. "Conscience looks backward and judges past actions, inducing that kind of dissatisfaction which if weak we call regret, and if severe, remorse" (Darwin, I. 91).

Remorse is easily explained. If by means of the internal rubbing of the atoms there is any grating, the result is disapproval ; if the rubbing is smooth and oily, the result is the approval of conscience. The disapproval if moderate is regret ; but if the grating is extremely severe, threatening to grind the atoms to powder, the result is remorse.

has been so consistently followed as actually to make men fanatical enough to become martyrs for the sake of truth and right, though, for the life of them, they could not see just what use or happiness was to be evolved from their torments.

It is a fatal objection to this theory that it does not base morality on the senses, but on notions of God and immortality, and on other invisible and immaterial objects. But aside from this unphilosophic and un-scientific procedure, how can right for its own sake be discovered as a principle of brutes, when probably not even its conception can be found in those who have demonstrated the moral character of animals? If men who hold this inconvenient theory have a sublime faith that the right will eventually result in the greatest happiness and prove itself of the greatest utility, why do they not invert the process and make the pleasur-able the right? If the right is useful, then the useful is right. Right is but the seed which if planted will grow into the fruit of usefulness and happiness. But the fruit is always the same as the seed whence it sprang; therefore the useful and the pleasurable is the same as the right. That's logic. Some bigot might say: "But the right must be planted in order that the useful and the pleasurable may spring from it; and all we have to do is the right and let the results, which are not in our power, take care of themselves." This, however, is but a theological bias, and does not rest on approved modern logic. Instead of the labori-ous process of planting and of long, impatient waiting for the tedious growth, the wise man prefers to pluck the fruit at once. Since right and truth and goodness exist solely for the sake of happiness, why not just take the happiness and let the conditions take care of themselves ?

The agreeable as the supreme rule of ethics—what more can be desired ? Before choosing, a man need only ask, Is it useful ? is it pleasurable ? The affirmative answer always gives the *ought*. But useful and agreeable to whom ? Of course to the doer, others being taken into account also so far as required by his interests. This is the true basis of social ethics. Sometimes, however, it is advantageous to adorn naked truth with becoming drapery ; circumlocutions and involutions were not intended for naught ; and selfishness—that black plague of society—will be robbed of its damnable hideousness by covering it with social instincts and altruistic notions. Materialism loathes all that is base and selfish ; and with its exalted views and refined means it strives to promote the divinest ends. Those who have learned by experience that it is to their own interest to treat others well, or whose emotions impel them irresistibly to deeds of kindness, have the generous altruistic conception and are free from the taint of selfishness. In its modern acceptation, selfishness consists of the conviction that it is to our advantage to ignore others, when it is really promotive of our interests to take them into account.

There is a strong flavor of folly in the objections which have been urged against this agreeable morality. It has been absurdly claimed that it robs a man of his noblest elements ; that it subordinates truth and right ; that it undermines conscience ; that it destroys the spirit of sacrifice, makes patriotism impossible, kills all disinterested emotions, and puts sociology on

the basis of swine-generosity. But this is purely a
matter of taste, to which all morality will soon be
reduced. Science deals solely with truth, and has
nothing to do with the exaltation or debasement of
man. Still, materialism unhesitatingly declares that
a man's noblest elements must necessarily be those
which harmonize him with the other ethical animals
and exalt him into unison with the rest of matter.
The fact that our moral basis is in harmony with natural and sexual selection, modern evolution, and
similar equally well-established hypotheses, speaks
volumes in its favor and demonstrates its truth. You
cannot degrade it by calling it kitchen-morality or
hog-ethics. It is so sublime just because the whole
animal creation is controlled by its principles. Everywhere the agreeable and the useful is the rule. The
strong devours the weak, or pushes it out of the way,
or tramples it under foot. The anthropoid animals
adopt the rule that to the victors belong the spoils—a
profound ethical principle! If the strong sees fit to
share his booty, that's his own business. Being controlled by altruistic sentiments, the brute is by no
means selfish, but shares its prey with its nearest kin
or a favorite companion; and when it feels like it the
brute is generous. Might makes right, inclination
constitutes generosity. The brute-mother submits to
hunger and other suffering for her offspring, being
forced to do so by her ethical instincts. This is social
morality highly developed.

The virtue of brutes is by no means limited to generosity. Mr. Darwin * says: "A great dog scorns

* I. 42.

the snarling of a little dog, and this may be called magnanimity." Why not? It will not be a slander on the dog. Some may find it difficult to put themselves in place of dogs; but great ones no doubt feel scorn at the snarling of pups. The dictionaries at my command do not indeed make scorn synonymous with magnanimity, since very perversely something magnanimous clings to the word in its various definitions. But this is a small matter. After properly exalting or debasing a subject, the word expressing it will speedily adapt itself to the new sense.

The materialistic rule of the supremacy of the useful and the pleasurable is a law of nature, and man is as completely under its control as the brute. The survival of the fittest is the corner-stone of ethics, and should be made the aim of legislation. We shall soon be sufficiently enlightened to overcome the folly of erecting institutions for those who are unable to take care of themselves. Nature has branded the weak, and sickly, and aged, and imbecile, and maimed, as unfit to live; and it is fighting against nature's laws to prolong their useless lives. The money wasted on them might be used for the healthy and strong, and thus humanity would be vastly improved. Those who are of no use to a community should be permitted, and aided, to die peacefully; by and by, legal enactments ridding the community of this wretched burden will become popular; then a state can become a paradise. Swift's proposal for the relief of Ireland was barbarous, because it proposed the indiscriminate slaughter of children; but the ethically agreeable requires that only the useless ones be put out of the way, together with all other persons who are a burden.

Why not? Sentiment? Social affection? Outrage public feeling? Wait a little. Soon we shall be
sufficiently advanced. Our feelings are already undergoing the proper training. Let the law of nature
once be fully recognized and it is done. We shall
not need the example of savages, or the teaching of
Greek sages, to square our hearts and our minds with
the demands of matter and the primal law of all animals. Every appeal to the rights of the individual
will properly be laughed to scorn after pleasure has
become the highest morality.

He who is physically the strongest is lord; that was
nature's intention, and it made him the strongest in
order that he might protect himself against the weak
and use them to minister to his pleasure; and that
man is blamable if he fails to appreciate and use his
endowments. The truly great men in all ages have
recognized this principle, and some had the moral
courage to use millions of persons for the attainment
of their personal ends. Nature ordains some to be
tyrants, others to be slaves. Women are weaker than
men; the moral law therefore teaches that they shall
be held in subjection and degradation if the lord of
creation so decides.

Danger of selfishness? Man can be saved from it
by studying the animals which feed, protect, carry,
lick, caress, and amuse their children; which herd
together to cultivate their social natures; and which
transmit their developed morality to their offspring.
Being free from all bias, and shams, and hypocrisies,
they reveal nature in its virgin purity. When the
lion is hungry he puts his moral law into practice vigorously, losing no time in weighing foolish scruples,

nature having endowed him with instincts which
enable him to go to work conscientiously as well as
with decency and dispatch. He knows that the survival of the fittest means himself, and acts on the
principle that the race of life is reduced to a question
of speed, and the battle of life to the problem of
strength and weapons and skill.

The next great epoch in ethical progress will be inaugurated by making the study of animal virtue the
basis of human morality. The reformer who takes
the lead in this movement will find valuable material
in popular writers of the day, some of whom have
already attained the high standard of refined brutes.

By getting the lowest conception of ethics we learn
its true character. Dealing largely with motives, we
must study it in animals, whose motives are so much
better understood than our own. But in order to understand morality perfectly, we must get behind it to
something from which it is supposed to have sprung.
No investigation is fashionably thorough or profound
unless it lands one in mystery and explains the known
by the unknowable. Our modern divers sink to unfathomable depths, and there feel at home and move
about freely. It is not enough to follow the roots to
their ultimate fibres in order to learn the nature of the
tree ; we must dig deeper ; and if we find a dry and
rotten stick below the roots, we know that it must
have been the original stock from which the tree
sprang.

You do not see the likeness between the stick and
the tree ? That is of no significance whatever. The
tree sprang from something ; that something was in
the earth, and it must still be there ; the stick was

found there, and its location cannot be explained
unless we suppose that it was the original stock from
which the tree grew. The difference between the
two ? Evolution !

By some magic, analogies are now seen where formerly none were found. As a consequence, words are
undergoing a remarkable transformation in common
with all other things. Men are bewildered and lost
when in the old familiar words they no longer find
the old familiar sense. Conscience is simply the product of a mathematical calculation. By reflecting on
his past conduct a man becomes dissatisfied with the
result. " Consequently he resolves to act differently
for the future—and this is conscience" *—not the
obsolete kind, but the latest evolvement. It is mere
pastime after this to find the *ought* in brutes. The
words quoted are followed by these : " Any instinct
which is permanently stronger, or more enduring than
another, gives rise to a feeling which we express by
saying that it ought to be obeyed. A pointer dog, if
able to reflect on his past conduct, would say to himself, ' 1 ought (as, indeed, we say of him) to have
pointed at that hare, and not have yielded to the passing temptation of hunting it.' " As the poor dog cannot say the *ought*, we say it for him and for all other
brutes. That's a modern privilege. The feelings
which they cannot understand we generously interpret
for them. With our powers more evolved than theirs,
we put ourselves in their place and interpret the animal humanly. And not an animal rises to protest, or
to prove the interpretation false !

* " Descent of Man," II. 392.

Any instinct may create the *ought*. But why stop with animals? The tree *ought* to grow in a favorable season. Words are very patient, as much so as the atoms from which they have grown. And who can object if they, in the whirl of evolution, are made to express thoughts and emotions and volitions which, according to former ages, ought to have been expressed in different terms? The age will gradually be evolved up to the new terminology, and will soon move on the level of those conceptions which are the inspiration of final science. The loss of old and cherished notions, like the loss of dear friends, may cause a pang at first; but human nature can bear much, and by and by we shall adapt ourselves to the new order of things, of which we ourselves shall be a part.

Some have been alarmed at the data of ethics furnished by the progressive evolution of the atoms, fearing that they might involve principles which are destructive of all humanity. This is merely a lack of appreciation or the result of religious prejudice. Morality of the old style is perishing; and the feeble kicks of its death-struggle will not hurt the young and vigorous heir of its place and fortunes. The highest principles and sublimest systems have ever been subject to the most marked opposition; and even the final ethics of materialism do not escape calumny. And yet was ever ice more chaste, or snow more pure?

Büchner's familiarity with materialism gives weight to the following: "Scientific materialism and the materialism of life are as distinct as heaven and earth, and it is only malice or narrowness which can confound them." A theoretical materialist proves his consistency by being a practical idealist. With the

grossest conceptions he is the most refined of spiritualists.   His system is of the earth, and he knows that
there is nothing but the earthy ; but practically he is
as far from that system as heaven is from earth—he is
heavenly and divine.   Between the earth and heaven
of materialism of course a great gulf is fixed.   Certainly the distinction between theoretical and practical
materialism is fully equal to the difference between a
materialist's earth and heaven !

    His ethics will teach the materialist that he is work-
ing for himself while promoting the interests of society
and the State.   That good, true, and honest moralist,
Iago, understood this perfectly.

> " Others there are
> Who, trimm'd in forms and visages of duty,
> Keep yet their hearts attending on themselves,
> And, throwing but shows of service on their lords,
> Do well thrive by them, and when they have lin'd their coats,
> Do themselves homage : these fellows have some soul ;
> And such a one do I profess myself."

With the spirit of useful morality, he faithfully
follows the Moor.

> " In following him I follow but myself ;
> Heaven is my judge, not I for love and duty,
> But seeming so for my peculiar end."

As the spiritual is evolved from the material, so
right is evolved from the pleasurable.   By serving
himself a man blesses others ; therefore he serves
others merely to serve himself.   It is as easy to evolve
generosity from selfishness as spirit from matter ; and
disinterested emotions, if they still exist, are evolved
from interested ones.   The social instincts of the

theoretical materialist, his feeling for his kin, his notions of useful and pleasureable decency and re-spectability, are his titles to nobility, and make him a moral hero. Men who are always ready to become martyrs, if it is to their interest, and to make martyrs of others, if it increases their pleasure, are our best citizens. This spirit of sacrifice constitutes the saints of the earth. Genuine utilitarians, from Alexander to Napoleon, prosecuted their schemes on a scale of mag-nificent generosity.

The truly materialistic moralist abhors everything which is calculated to lower him in the estimation of others, since this degradation is painful to him. While his conscience is tender it will be wrong for him to do anything in private which can cause him remorse ; but after his moral sense has overcome its sentimental stage, he will attain greater freedom and be able to pursue the useful and pleasurable regardless of con-science, and, after proper discipline, even with its ap-proval. In fact, since conscience is the highest faculty in man, there is no other which is more plastic, more adaptable to occasions and circumstances, more yield-ing or more stern, as the case may demand. Like all other law, the moral one thus proves itself a thing for use. It can be in a solid, a fluid, or in a gaseous state ; it can sleep or wake ; like a needle on a pivot, or like a weathercock, it can point in any direction ; so that, taken all in all, it is the most serviceable, the most pliable, and the most convenient of all the en-dowments of men and other animals, and its skilful use is the great art in a moral life. It was never in-tended to be " a canker," and never is in its normal state in brutes. Poets and priests and novelists make

it a tormentor, and depict it as hell instead of heaven.
The philosopher who avails himself of its elastic properties, and scorns to be its slave, is free from its re-
proaches.   Let him but persuade himself that he is
what he is by a necessity of nature ; then all responsibility will vanish, remorse will cease, and deep, heavenly peace will hallow his soul.   Nature's great poet
knew that this is the way to heaven.   The loving
Edmund soliloquizes : " This is the excellent foppery
of the world, that when we are sick in fortune (often
the surfeit of our own behavior), we make guilty of
our disasters the sun, the moon, and stars, as if we
were villains on necessity ; fools by heavenly compul-
sion ; knaves, thieves, and treachers by spherical predominance ; drunkards, liars, and adulterers by an
enforced obedience of planetary influence ; and all that
we are evil in by a divine thrusting on : an admirable
evasion of whore-master man, to lay his goatish disposition on the charge of a star !"   Our Edmunds are
not guilty of this " evasion."   Instead of stars and
planets, and " divine thrusting on," they go back scientifically to the atoms and necessary laws, and thus
secure the morality of the bastard.

Whoever has the wisdom to make inclination the
guide of his life, will find pleasure in many things
(provided they are not discovered), which with the old
views of conscience would cause pain.   He will know
no fear but the disapproval of his fellow-men.   All
his interests lie this side of the grave—no man in his
right mind any longer risking a wager on another life.

This world, this only, is man's pasture.   What a
man *seems* is the great desideratum.   The secret.
securely locked in the breast, will die forever with its

possessor. If a rock-crystal can be so cut as to look like a diamond, is it not just as good ? The glitter is the essence. It is prudent for a man to appear virtuous, and honest, and charitable, and public-spirited ; and though he were the devil incarnate, his seeming would have its reward.

However, those who still remember the thing may regret the decay and death of the old conscience ; it is doomed. Even in a rudimentary stage it is uncommon and exceedingly unpopular. Restraints will soon be consigned wholly to the vulgar. And every man of culture will be able to say from his heart : " As to conscience and nasty morals, I have as few drawbacks upon my pleasures as any man of quality in England ; in those I am not at least vulgar."

Our system of materialistic morals is absolutely perfect, and is intended for perfect men. A man whose knowledge is absolute sees the end from the beginning, and consequently knows what is ultimately, not merely for the present, useful and pleasurable. The " ultimately," of course, always falls in this life ; and to make sure of it, the sooner it comes the better. Instinctively he knows that unless the greatest happiness flows from the greatest virtue the atoms must somehow be in conflict with one another and self-destructive. Therefore he eagerly seizes the pleasurable in order ultimately to promote the right.

The opponents of our materialistic utilitarian ethics wholly pervert the true, and natural, order of things when they regard truth and right as absolutely fixed and independent of man, a standard which his inclination cannot affect. Their error is equally great when they view the pleasurable as relative, depending on

the subject as taste on the palate or hearing on the
ear. These perversions are, however, met by the new
and improved view of conscience, which does not
make it a tool of the right, but its lord, governing the
right as it likes, and thus making it an ornament
worthy of a free and noble soul. The right is variable, shifting with the wind, while the useful and
pleasurable are absolutely fixed—the pleasurable being
what agrees with my inclinations, and the useful that
which gratifies the inclinations or promotes my pleasures. These are therefore supreme ; all right depends
on them, and their choice is final. The man with perfect knowledge, with a perfect heart, and with a perfect will never makes a mistake in choosing them ;
but the right, the true, and the good are able to take
care of themselves. Philosophers have always been
controlled by utilitarian morals ; it increased Bacon's
wealth ; it sweetened the disposition of Schopenhauer ;
and it evolved all the morals possessed by materialists.

With the unphilosophic mind it is otherwise, neither
being controlled by intricate dialectics nor sublimated
by refined subtleties. The stupid frequently exhibit
a sad and fatal directness, wholly at variance with
healthy circumlocution and shrewd philosophic reserve. Where the sluggish mind and untutored conscience discern right and wrong, truth and error, the
cultured man demonstrates that these are only different in degree, not in kind ; and diving to the bottom
of error and wrong, he seizes the soul of their truth
and right, and proves that this soul is the essence of
right and wrong, which are but its body. While irre-
deemable stupidity speaks what it thinks and acts as it
feels, true wisdom refines the speech into propriety

and whittles the feelings, as far as expressed, down to the point of respectability.

There are many hopeful signs that the principles of materialistic ethics will soon become universal. Then the mask will be thrown aside, and that will be done openly which is now done only in secret. When that new moral era is inaugurated, society will return to a state of nature in a sense of which Rousseau never dreamed. All crimes will cease after it has been proved that they are but physical diseases, or evolutions of improper organizations, or mistaken notions of happiness. Prisons, a relic of barbarous ages, will be converted into hospitals and asylums, until society has been sufficiently developed to let natural selection dispose of all who are no longer fit to live. In that blessed age moral teachers will not be needed, but can be transmuted into insane doctors. We have already brought mind down to matter, and morals must speedily follow. Then vice and all moral perversity will be shown to result from a disordered tissue of the nerves ; from the improper overlapping of the folds of the brain ; from the predominance of the white, or gray, substance of the brain, or from the increase or decrease of its phosphorus ; from the lack of rhythm in the beat of the heart and some pulse ; or from the irregularity of the vibration of atoms in the ideas ; or from some other equally rational physical cause.

It cannot be too emphatically stated that, aside from material causes, there is absolutely nothing in vice and crime but an error of judgment respecting the nature of the pleasurable ; indeed, this very error is also purely physical. Garfield's assassin professed to believe his victim in the way of the public welfare, and as no foolish notion of right restrained him from pursuing his utilitarian ethics, he shot the President. It took a year of imprisonment and his experience on the gallows to convince him that even the most enlightened nations have not yet learned to regard a man's whims as the rule of right. A Berlin murderer had the same pleasurable notion of morality, without scruples as to the ability of right to take care of itself. Loving a woman whom he wanted to marry, he hung his wife and three children during the silent watches of the night. If it had not been for the court he might never have discovered that his notion of pleasure was a mistake ; indeed, had the law not interfered, the fourfold murder would not have been a mistake or a crime ! Before long, the law and courts of justice and such individuals will be in perfect harmony. The horrors which fill our papers are regarded as wicked only by those who cling to the exploded theological notion of sin—that foolish and diabolical myth which our progressive age is wiping from the face of the earth, excepting, perhaps, a few hysteric brains, sentimental hearts, and soft consciences.

I thought of saying a word about the dread of punishment hereafter, and the hope of reward, as motives of conduct ; but as no one is any longer affected by these it is unnecessary. All justice is meted out here ; and in the scramble for reward each one must see to it that he secures his prize as soon as possible, otherwise it may escape him altogether. To the innocent victim who is murdered, and to his murderer who ends on the gallows, death ends all. The torture thus inflicted on the innocent is his reward—a reward perhaps a thousandfold more intense in lingering agony than that inflicted on the assassin. That's even-handed justice !

It is a pity that the rabble have not yet learned that theoretical materialism does not lead to the practical. When the useful and the agreeable are theoretically adopted as the sole aim of life, the vulgar herd are too stupid to see that the practical aim should be totally different ; and in their madness they foolishly practise what they profess. For the life of them they do not see the need of letting a favored few possess the houses and lands and money of the country, while they themselves live in poverty and wretchedness ! The wealth of the millionaire, they argue, would be more useful and confer greater pleasure by distribution ; hence they proceed to do it, if they can, though it may cost the owner's life. These vandals argue that if there is no God, no immortality, no retribution, then there is nothing to fear hereafter ; and their conscience helps them to help themselves to some other man's property—a striking illustration of the hopelessly illogical state of the uncultivated ! We can only save them from their mistake by convincing them that no man can enjoy what he has not earned, and that property cannot be earned by robbery and murder. But this lesson they may prefer to learn experimentally rather than theoretically. Of course the dangers of communism will cease after they have learned that lesson ! But if this cannot somehow be demonstrated into them, we may find it necessary to take them to hospitals and asylums to be cured, though the time may soon come when the larger part of the inhabitants would have to be put into these institutions. If the masses ever get the theory that the ethical is the pleasurable, firmly rooted in their minds and hearts, practical scruples will soon vanish.   Nihilism, Social- ism, and Communism will then speedily solve all po- litical and social problems on the principle of the sur- vival of the fittest.   In that blessed era human moral- ity will be evolved to the ethics of the brutes.

CHAPTER IX.

"Mathematicians—I do not mean the inventors and geniuses among them, whom I honor, but the demonstrators of others' inventions, who are ten times duller and prouder than a damned poet—have a strange aversion to everything that smacks of religion."—WARBURTON.

"It is likewise proposed as a great advantage to the public that if we once discard the system of the gospel, all religion will of course be banished forever ; and consequently along with it those grievous prejudices of education, which, under the names of virtue, conscience, honor, justice, and the like, are so apt to disturb the peace of human minds, and the notions whereof are so hard to be eradicated, by right reason, or free-thinking."—SWIFT.

FORMERLY religion was an invention of priests to enable them to hoodwink the masses. But it seemed unaccountable that a deception should last so long, and should have fooled so many enlightened persons in former ages. This pious fraud is, therefore, no longer the origin of religion. It now had its source in dreams and shadows, in somnambulism, or the sight of a corpse, or in something else, which convinced primitive man that there is another self besides the body. For giving religion this origin, the world is mainly indebted to Mr. Herbert Spencer. Whatever else may be doubtful, it is certain that religion must have originated in mistake and superstition, just as it has been promoted mainly by these. Here is a field in which scientific inventions are still possible. Ghosts are of special significance; the more horrible, the more serviceable in frightening religion into men. Since ghosts can be conjured up at pleasure, they might be utilized as the basis for the numerous dreams in Mr. Spencer's books.

The psychological element in religion may be wholly ignored, while all the emphasis is placed on outward suggestions. The inner adaptation to spirituality is of no importance if we can get the environment to do everything. Since our religious nature is best learned from brutes, I cannot understand what Jevons ("Principles of Science") means by the following : " Our own hopes and wishes and determinations are the most undoubted phenomena within the space of consciousness. If men do act, feel, and live as if they were not merely the brief products of a casual conjunction of atoms, but the instruments of a far-reaching purpose, are we to record all other phenomena and pass over these ? We investigate the instincts of the ant and the bee and the beaver, and discover that they are led by an inscrutable agency to work toward a distant purpose. Let us be faithful to our scientific method, and investigate all those instincts of the human mind by which man is led to work as if the approval of a Higher Being were the aim of life."

Such writers forget that " the instincts of the ant and the bee and beaver" are far more important than those of the soul ; for the instincts of animals can be of service in evolving human instincts ; but of what earthly use are the instincts of man ? Can any animal traits be traced to them ?

The nature of the soul has absolutely nothing to do with the origin of religion ; it is a product of man's environment. After we have succeeded in making the first religious suggestions to our infant race by means of ghosts and somnambulism, we can let the mysteries of life and nature help men to imagine a great but unseen power behind phenomena ; thus all that could be fancied but not explained suggested a deity. Then, as ever since, the Inconceivable was the fruitful source of reverence, and it is the fountain whence all known religions have sprung.

There are also other origins of religion, as may be learned by studying other scientific writers. Since, however, even the newest theories have become somewhat insipid, and with their novelty have lost their attraction and intrinsic value, it is about time for some new inventions to be started. Fresh novels must take the place of the old and stale ones, which no person cares to read twice ; the new romance will be superseded by the newest, provided it is wild and fantastic enough. Such things must be adapted to the market for which they are made.

As it is possible to get knowledge from mere sensation without wasting a thought on the peculiarity of the mind, so we can, perhaps, get religion altogether from the environment without considering the religious element in man himself. Once admit that man has a religious nature, or a religious sentiment, or a spiritual faculty, or anything else which makes religion a necessity, and it will be hard to get rid of religion. Even in fiction the credulity must not be too severely strained, but the imagination must be disciplined into conformity with human life. It is, therefore, not advisable to put all the creative energy in the environment ; at least, this much of the genesis of religion

might be made human : that man is susceptible to religious impressions from the external creative energy.

The struggle for existence has not yet succeeded in
accounting for all existing religions, especially since
it has been proved that we can perhaps exist as well
without as with religion.   This struggle somehow always gets along best when it has the least to do with
ideals, thus proving their worthlessness.   Natural selection finds it hard to blossom into the poetry from the
Hebrew bards, and Homer, down to Longfellow, and
Tennyson ; into the mysticism of Tauler and Boehme ;
and into the idealism of Berkeley and Fichte.   Even
in a hot-house, with all the manure of the stalls, it is
difficult to develop the survival of the fittest into spiritual religion.   Strange that matter so develops itself
in man that it strives to free itself from matter, and to
rise above it to something not enslaved by its stern
necessity ! If the struggle for existence develops
these things which have nothing to do with our purely
material existence, but rather antagonize it, then may
it not also, in other cases, produce not the thing aimed
at, but its opposite ?   Great, however, as the difficulties seem, they are only apparent.   We have here
another illustration of the remarkable tendency of
matter to develop itself into opposite and contradictory
characteristics.   Religion is, of course, the offspring
of natural selection, and we have no doubt that some
time in the future this opinion will find confirmation.
If any religion were not thus produced, it would be
worthless, and its discussion would not deserve our
consideration, unless perhaps we can explain it by
sexual selection.

By applying the usual methods of spiritual material-

ism it will become self-evident that religion is not
peculiar to man, but, like morality, is shared by the
other animals. A suitable definition of religion is of
course essential. Define it so as not to leave in it
anything peculiar, and it can then be proved not to be
peculiar to man. Fortunately, Mr. Vogt has anticipated my conclusion : " I verily do not know how to
find a reason for attaching to the whole human family
religion as an altogether peculiar characteristic." In
the religion here considered fear is an essential element, and we can afford to use it lavishly. The same
spiritual authority says : " The stupid idiot takes no
notice whatever of thunder ; the simpleton fears it
as a mighty natural phenomenon whose cause he cannot
discover ; out of the unknown x the heathen develops a god of thunder ; the believing Christian lets
his God thunder ; and the intelligent man who knows
anything of physics does his own thundering and
lightning, if he has the necessary apparatus." The
scientist and the simpleton recognize as a " natural
phenomenon" what the Christian and heathen recognize as divine ; and religion was probably communicated by thunder, just as morality was inculcated by
snarling and flogging.

With special pleasure I find that my favorite animal
can be put to a spiritual use—namely, to prove that the
religious germ is not peculiarly human. Again, Professor Vogt is my authority. " The dog is evidently
afraid of ghosts, just as much as the inhabitants of
Bretagne or of the Basque provinces. Every strange
phenomenon respecting which his nose cannot give
him the proper knowledge leads even the most courageous dog to give expression to the most senseless

fear.   I know a small forest, which the peasants
were convinced that, at night, was inhabited by a
fiery man ; and in proof of the existence of this fiery
sprite, they affirmed that after dark the dogs were
afraid in this forest, and that such dogs as had once
been in it at night could not be induced to re-enter,
even by beating.   The ghost, whose neighborhood a
dog in other respects courageous did not dare to ap-
proach, even in company with my father, his master,
was the white, rotten trunk of a tree, which cast a glim-
mer in the dark.   The fear of the supernatural, of the
unknown, which is the germ of religious conceptions,
is found in our intelligent domestic animals—the dog
and the horse—in a highly developed degree.   The
germ of these conceptions, as of so many others, is
only further developed by man, is worked up into a
system, into faith.''

It is not quite clear how the fear of the rotten trunk
leads to the conclusion that dogs and horses fear '' the
supernatural ;'' but that is owing to the acuteness of
the reasoning, and does not alter the fact.   For thousands of years, philosophers have been studying profoundly the origin of religion without solving the
problem, and behold the Zürich professor settles it
without even an effort at thought !   It would be un-
just to blame him for having no notion of religion, except such as can be developed from germs found in
dogs, since the basest conception of religion fully reveals its essence.   Man still retains the prerogative of
developing this '' senseless fear'' '' into a system, into
faith.''   It is a peculiarity of evolution that it always
lands a man in error and superstition when it develops
him far beyond the brutes.   How blessed the dog,

that he can end his religion with his fear, and is not obliged, like silly man, to develop it into a system of superstitious faith !

I was still pondering the question, how the dog evolved the rotten trunk into "the supernatural, the unknown," when Mr. Darwin came to my help. "The tendency in savages to imagine that natural objects and agencies are animated by spiritual or living essences is perhaps illustrated by a little fact which I once noticed : my dog, a full-grown and very sensible animal, was lying on the lawn during a hot and still day ; but at a little distance a slight breeze occasionally moved an open parasol, which would have been wholly disregarded by the dog had any one stood near it. As it was, every time that the parasol slightly moved the dog growled fiercely and barked.- He must, I think, have reasoned to himself in a rapid and unconscious manner, that movement without any apparent cause indicated the presence of some strange living agent, and no stranger had a right to be on his territory." *

According to the present status of the psychology of dogs, it is impossible to tell just what this dog thought and felt, and how he reasoned. In rare cases even the motives of men may be misinterpreted. But since the dog belonged to Mr. Darwin, he undoubtedly has a right to give an authoritative interpretation of the conduct of the animal. If brutes can help us to understand our religion, why not help dog-consciousness by interpreting into it our human emotions and thoughts ?

* I. 67.

Having reached this stage in our science of religion, I remark that it is a peculiarity of the religious germ in dogs and horses that it never develops into religion —another providential evidence that there is no design in nature. Would an intelligent designer create so many germs in vain? Should one still imagine that this is not the tap-root of religion, we have a fact which settles it scientifically : the religious germ of dogs develops into religion in man on account of his peculiar environment. Perhaps it is a slander on brutes to declare that they have no religion ; for has it not been discovered " that a dog looks on his master as a god "? Those who are surprised to find the religious germ in dogs and horses rather than in man's nearer kin, the ape, need but reflect that a characteristic sometimes leaps from a grandparent to a grandchild. But there is no doubt that *this* religious germ can also be found in monkeys.

Religions are all natural and material, the evolution of physical laws. The poor dog cannot avoid that senseless fear which terrifies him into a recognition of the supernatural ; nor can man help it that in him matter develops this fear into a system of faith. In the dog as well as in man the supernatural is the product of atomic development.

Yielding to my necessity, I am forced to give this definition : *Religion is an affinity for the highest.* Affinity is thus seen to be the essential element of religion; wherever it is found, religion exists, and wherever it is absent there is no religion ; hence all affinities are links in the development of religion. If its germ is found in animals, then the germ of that germ is found in inorganic matter, and the germ of that must be in the atoms. My view of religion has this advantage over others : it enables me to go back farther and to trace its origin to the ultimate source. In the atoms, religion is seen in their attractive power ; their repulsion is their irreligious element. Chemical molecules unite in definite proportions ; this proportional affinity is their religion. A plant takes from soil and air and sunlight the elements which its affinity attracts, and this constitutes the religion of vegetable life. In animals this affinity is still more marked, and is quite various. In those which are united into an undifferentiated mass the affinity is palpable. Two animals may be so religiously attached as to form but one ; when cut in two, each irreligiously walks off. In the canine species the affinity is often touching, their attachments being peculiarly strong, as evinced by licking the hand that feeds them, and in other equally religious acts.

It has already been shown that in man necessity has, by a transformation of forces, been converted into freedom—a freedom which depends on the peculiar shape, motion, and combination of the atoms. This freedom, which has been forced on man, gives him the privilege of choosing his religion, which accounts for the variety in faith. Here, as in other departments of nature, there are no differences of species and genera, but only varieties of the same kind. The doctrine of transmutation receives wonderful confirmation from religion. Thus a man may pass from Heathenism to Mohammedanism, thence to Judaism, Christianity, and Agnosticism, and thence to Atheism ; or he may begin with Atheism and end with Heathenism. There is, therefore, either no difference of species in relig-

ion, or, if there is, it does not interfere with the
transmutation of species ; and in either case the doctrine of transmutation is established.   Thus, in passing
from the lowest to the highest form—from Heathenism to Atheism—it is proved that there is either no
difference in kind, or that in spite of it the passage
from the one to the other is perfectly easy and natural.

Spiritual materialism, as might be inferred from the
adjective, is devoutly religious, but withal tolerant
and extremely liberal.   If one admits that there is
nothing but matter and its laws, he is at liberty to
choose whatever religion he pleases.   When Mr. Darwin says that the question respecting the existence of
a Creator and Ruler of the universe "has been answered in the affirmative by the highest intellects that
have ever lived," he can hardly have included the
present generation ; for to the highest intellects now
atoms are the creators and laws the rulers of the
universe.

A spiritual materialist may find it prudent not to
deny the possibility of the existence of something besides matter, provided no practical inferences are
drawn.   This depends entirely on the community in
which he resides.   Since he knows that there is nothing but atoms he cannot really be an agnostic, especially since even Christians admit that religion is full
of mystery.   A man may be an agnostic, fully admitting that the highest realm cannot be known so perfectly as a materialist knows the atoms ; nevertheless,
he may have a conviction which is as firm as knowledge ; he may have an immovable faith, may be a devout worshipper of something unseen, and may live
as if there really were something beyond matter.

This is superstition, and that no spiritual materialist can tolerate. But a higher form of Agnosticism has been evolved in recent times which he may find it convenient to adopt, though he need not for this reason class himself with those who are really, and at heart, agnostics.

Modern agnosticism may be called religious Know-Nothingism. The principal factors in its evolution are Kant, Hamilton, Mansel, Herbert Spencer ; but with a difference. Kant showed that the speculative reason can find no firm basis for religion, and can never demonstrate the existence of God, Freedom, and Immortality. He, however, did not regard this as a serious objection, since the " primacy," or supremacy, belongs to the " practical " reason, which gives an immovable basis for religion and morality. Speculative agnosticism can, however, claim Kant as one of its forerunners by emphasizing some of his speculative conclusions and rejecting all his practical ones, a process perfectly legitimate when the sole aim is to find a basis for speculative agnosticism. Hamilton and Mansel have also furnished material which can be used to good advantage ; but they were not agnostics who can be followed by materialists, since they left room for faith. A genuine, scientific agnostic does not leave even a shadow of knowledge for belief, and some of them leave nothing but a sneer on which religion can build.

Mr. Spencer is the last and most important factor in the evolution of agnosticism, and as such is worthy of profound study. His religion is deposited in his " First Principles," a philosophic and scientific work based on the deductive method. There are also traces

of the inductive method, and sometimes there is considerable of a mixture of both ; frequently, however,
the method is neither deductive nor inductive, but
original and peculiarly Spencerian. The first part,
which chiefly concerns us here, has some facts
sprinkled in between the hypotheses, and fiction
enough to give the work a popular flavor. "The
Unknowable" is the first subject discussed, an incom-
parable arrangement full of scientific advantages. If
he had begun with "The Knowable," he would probably never have discovered the Unknowable, which
might then have remained unknown forever. After
the "Synthetic Philosophy" has discovered and limited
the unknowable, and given all its characteristic marks,
it finds it easy to deduce the knowable, which consists
simply of what is left after the science of the unknowable is finished.

· Mr. Spencer begins his knowledge of the unknowable with these words : "We too often forget that
not only is there ' a soul of goodness in things evil,'
but very generally also a soul of truth in things
erroneous." Of course there is generally wheat where
there is chaff, and fire where there are ashes. The
reminder is of great importance, and very properly
begins the book ; and I confess that in reading Mr.
Spencer's works, and especially in pondering some of
his herculean conclusions, I have found comfort in
the knowledge that there *is* "a soul of truth in things
erroneous," even if we are unable to discover it.

In the interest of religion and science the author
proceeds to seek this "soul." Before he makes this
search, it is, of course, taken for granted that all religious opinions held till that time were false—they

were so many erroneous bodies which held a true soul.
These various bodies have but one soul, and this he
proceeds to extract—a process whose success depends
largely on the taste and skill of the dissector of the
bodies. Any one with ordinary ingenuity can find
just the soul he is looking for ; and consequently one
finds one soul, another quite a different one ; and
many find the soul altogether too subtle, and therefore cling to one of the numerous bodies. Mr. Spencer himself has attained considerable variety in his
discoveries. By putting together the various souls
found, the result will necessarily be the absolute soul,
which is of course the animating principle of the absolute Synthetic Philosophy. This will remain the
soul of truth until some future philosopher treats that
system as its author handles all other opinions. With
reasoning powers equal to those of Mr. Spencer, he
will perhaps find a soul of some kind.*

Kant, as well as Locke, subjected himself to a laborious examination of the nature of the human intellect
in order to determine its limits. But that was over
one hundred years ago, long before the crowning vic-

---

* Some may have wondered why, when the Prospectus of his
works was issued, in 1860, no book on logic was included ; wondered all the more because such a book would probably have been
the most interesting of the series. The omission is, however, a
merit instead of a fault, since there is so much in the system
which is more perfect without than with logic.

It has been said that the books of the Synthetic Philosophy are
valuable to the logician because they furnish illustrations of all
possible logical fallacies—illustrations of course intended for that
purpose by the author. However this may be, it is certain that
their variety and completeness in this respect are equalled by few
other philosophic works.

tories of modern philosophy. Mr. Spencer, on the other hand, first determines the limits of the human faculties, and then their nature ; thus he first limits the unknowable in his " First Principles," and long afterward determines the nature of the intellect in his " Principles of Psychology." The uninitiated may be unable to understand how the unknowable can be known before the limits of the mind or of the knowable have been fixed ; but nothing is easier. It is, in fact, not even necessary to make a distinction between the unknown and the unknowable, or to indicate the degrees of the knowable. Since the unknowable of one age may become the knowable of the next, it will avoid confusion if the unknowable is made eternally unknowable. Sharp distinctions may prove a fetter, and should therefore be avoided ; and a careful definition of the word *knowable* might completely convert the unknowable. So it is only necessary to define the unknowable as the Infinite, the Absolute ; this definition is then carefully defined, so as to exclude all possibility of putting anything intelligible into it ; and this is the unknowable. The definition of the unknowable proves that it has actually been found and is known ; then proof is given that no definition of it is possible, and thus the matter is settled.

If there were any doubt that the unknowable has really been discovered, it would be demonstrated away by Mr. Spencer's frequent and emphatic assertions that it is found. To make assurance doubly sure, he also gives some of its characteristics, which no one who studies them can fail to recognize. First of all, he demonstrates mathematically, by means of proper definitions, that we can know absolutely nothing

about it, except that it is absolutely unknowable. By
no possible effort of our faculties can we discover in
or on it any mark, or quality, or attribute, whatever ;
for as soon as anything distinctive is found in it—something which distinguishes it from anything else—it
loses its distinctive mark as the unknowable. Then
it is demonstrated that the unknowable really exists—
in fact, its existence is the most certain of all things.
Then it is shown that the unknowable is a power,
and, in fact, the greatest power in the universe. Not
only is it power, but the source of all other power ;
it is the First Cause. It is another peculiarity of the
unknowable that it manifests itself perpetually to our
consciousness ; and do what we may, we cannot rid
ourselves of its presence. By what marks the utterly
inconceivable, which has no marks, can persistently
manifest itself to our consciousness, is inconceivable,
except according to the peculiar "Psychology" of
the Synthetic Philosophy. There are degrees in the
consciousness of this unknowable. "Thus the consciousness of an Inscrutable Power manifested to us
through all phenomena has been growing ever clearer,
and must eventually be freed from its imperfections.
The certainty, on the one hand, that such a power exists, while, on the other hand, its nature transcends in-
tuition, and is beyond imagination, is the certainty
toward which intelligence has from the first been
progressing. To this conclusion Science inevitably
arrives as it reaches its confines, while to this conclusion Religion is irresistibly driven by criticism. And
satisfying as it does the demands of the most rigorous
logic at the same time that it gives the religious sentiment the widest possible sphere of action, it is the

conclusion we are bound to accept without reserve or qualification."

The absolute is absolutely unknowable ; but to the consciousness this inscrutable power is manifested through all phenomena ; the consciousness is ever growing clearer, and will eventually be freed from all imperfection ! The consciousness of this inscrutable power gives the religious sentiment the widest possible sphere of action—the limitless sphere of the unknowable. Inestimable privilege ! Religion thus has free play, and can soar in this absolute void as easily and delightfully as a bird can fly after the atmosphere which impedes its progress has been removed. How generous ! The knowable being abstracted, all that is left is relegated to religion. The infinite blank that remains "gives the religious sentiment the widest possible sphere of action."

Mr. Spencer has a variety of unknowables, and long practice has enabled him to show them off to best advantage. He takes peculiar pleasure in thrusting them on your attention when least expected and least desired. They seem to lie in ambush, anxiously waiting for the moment of action. But there is this peculiarity in his unknowables : some are for use, others for disuse. An unknowable can be made a seed from which the world develops, or it may be made utter emptiness. What a convenience ! Time, space, matter, force, are all unknowables. Mr. Spencer, as we have already seen, has labelled and shelved them as such. When you enter his variety shop, and ask for an article, he shows you its essence as unknowable, and by means of ingenious dilutions he manufactures the knowable to order. The essence is then bottled up and returned to the shelf for safe-keeping. Time, space, matter, force, are unknowable essences, which can be utilized by philosophy, and are indispensable for the evolution of evolution. What would the Synthetic Philosophy be without these unknowables? A form without content. When they are needed, it uses them freely and familiarly ; and whatever it cannot explain or does not suit its taste, can be bottled up with the unknowable essence. When necessary, the bottles are uncorked, and some of the spirit is permitted to exhale. This is especially the case when the knowable is to be explained, which is done by means of the Unknowable. The knowable can only be seen by putting it into the light of the unknowable. The Synthetic Philosophy modestly appropriates the entire region of the knowable to itself ; of the unknowable it also has the monopoly ; but so much of that as it cannot use is proved useless, and then magnanimously consecrated to religion ! The unknowable as the first cause cannot be used, except perhaps as a resting-place for weary philosophic thought, differing strikingly from the usefulness of matter and force as causes. The general law is, that the unknowable, so far as needed by modern philosophy, is of the utmost importance ; but so far as needed by religion it is altogether beyond our reach, and only fit to be thrust aside as worthless. A philosophy built on the unknowable is glorious ; but religion built on it would be contemptible if it were not so ridiculous.

Agnostic religion useless, then? That depends on the logic applied. Seriously viewed, yes. The absolutely unknowable is absolutely beyond reach, is nothing to us, and with it nothing can be done. I

mean as far as religion is concerned ; the logic of its
use for modern science is, of course, different. But
in another sense this religion is very serviceable. If
a man adopts it he can refer all religious questions to
this abyss, and there let them rest forever. No one
can prove him an atheist, for no one knows what he
is, least of all he himself. All charges, which in some
communities might be inconvenient, are false ; and
he can prove it by demonstrating that his religion
is nothing, and that, therefore, it can have nothing
objectionable.

After the unknowable as the religious basis had
been discovered, and described, by Mr. Spencer, he
put it safely into a corner ; and now men of fashionable culture need only read the label, or smell the
bottle, in order to learn that the contents are not their
affinity. After a matter has once been established by
a creative mind, it is not polite to work the whole
thing over again by original and profound thought.
Our age is blessed with a peculiar kind of ruminants :
the master swallows the food, and his disciples chew
the cud.

This religion is specially adapted to gentlemen of
refinement and scholarship, and there is nothing in it
to which the materialist can object. It will at least
enable him to fling back into the teeth of calumnia-
tors the charge that he has no religion. This philosophic and scientific spirituality is a great advance on
former superstitions and irreligious ages. Montes-
quieu once said, " There is no religion in England.
. . . If any one speaks of religion, everybody begins to laugh. A man happening to say, ' I believe
this as I believe an article of religion,' everybody

burst out laughing.'' Thanks to the unknowable, that frivolous spirit is banished.

A spiritual materialist who finds agnosticism too empty can easily construct a religion to meet his needs. Taking the religious basis of dreams and shadows and ghosts, he can evolve from these the substances which are the ground of his faith and hope. Of course he knows perfectly well that there is no reality behind the religious pictures which chase each other across the fancy ; he is, therefore, free to cherish those which are beautiful and rejoice the heart, while he rejects the dark and hideous ones which represent remorse and torments.

Lately a highly satisfactory species, called '' Natural Religion,'' was introduced into England. It is not quite clear why it should be labelled '' Natural,'' since all religions are equally the product of nature. If there is nothing but matter, the old logic would say that all religions are a creation or evolution of matter ; what popular, modern logicians would decide can only be known after they have tackled the question ; but I think they would hold in theory that all religions are evolutions of matter, while practically they would damn those religions they did not find congenial, and curse the adherents as if they were responsible for the products of the necessary laws of matter. It may be that the new species is called '' Natural,'' because its followers know that its objects are mere fancies and natural products, while others imagine their vagaries to be supernatural realities. Crazy folk, for instance, believe in the truth of their religious fancies, and worship accordingly ; but the natural religionist knows that religion is nonsense, and yet cherishes it as though

it were the highest wisdom ; thus he proves the
superiority of his natural spirituality over the insane
religion.

Natural Religion is fully conscious of itself, and
transforms all religious emotions and aspirations into
heartless reflection.   It is a jolly thing ; to those in-
fected with the old notions of religion it may seem like
irony, like a burlesque ; but its rollicking fun and de-
lightful fancies are necessary to keep away the pessimis-
tic spirit, which might otherwise breathe poison into its
heavenly pleasures.   With a sardonic smile, its happy
devotees look upon those who have not yet learned to regard their spiritual ideas as utterly empty—with which,
from the very nature of the case, nothing real can correspond.   Where the agnostic traces the outlines of the
unknowable, and gives all the characteristics of the
absolutely mysterious, natural religionists see behind
their fancies nothing but an infinite void—a vacuum,
in which even thought loses its gravity and fancy its
buoyancy.   While the agnostic is astounded by what
he does not know of religion almost as much as by
what he knows of everything else which he has
evolved from the unknowable, the natural religionist
is astounded that men do not see that religion is nothing but an idle tale ; and he is surprised that they re-
fuse to repeat it to themselves as true, after it has been
proved a fiction.   They cherish the most exalted
notion of God, and commend it as the acme of science,
philosophy, and poetry, and the consummation of all
longing and hope.   It is the ideal of religion because
it is nothing but idea.   How charming !   The atheist
can adopt it unhesitatingly, and may be the most devout of men ; and materialists, whether spiritual or

material, may be religious zealots, after attaining a
knowledge of the innocent emptiness of this grand
conception of Deity.

Natural religion has an immortality of the soul as
well as a God, and its votaries cherish with rapture
the conception of an endless existence of man's spirit.
Nothing but a conception, of course ; but need it be
less sublime because it represents nothing real ? What
a sphere of action this affords the imagination ! When
a man dies he is dead—his spirit as well as his body,
and that's the end of him. To imagine that anything
lives after a man is dead is too ridiculous for philosophic faith. It is one of the deepest joys of life that
the time will come when we shall be blessed with un-
consciousness. Büchner very properly regards the
idea of immortality as probably the most horrible
which human fancy could invent !

What is true of God and immortality is true of
every other object of religion : it is absolutely nothing
but a notion. Religion is a mere projection of a man's
brains, an objectifying of himself, and nothing else.
He sees the reflections from the mirror of his consciousness, and if blessed with modern wisdom, he
knows that they are simply empty images thrown off by
movements of the molecules of his brain ; lacking this
wisdom, he will imagine them supernatural realities.
The believer who worships religious objects worships
himself or his fancies. This was long ago stated by
Feuerbach and confirmed by Strauss. They knew that
religion consists of ghosts, and they treated it accordingly. The proposition to treat these shadows as substances would have seemed to them the height of folly.
Our modern philosophers are much more evolved.

and make some form of religion desirable. He cannot always succeed in making his heart the adamant
which feels neither longing, nor hope, nor love, nor
fear. Sometimes his rebellious mind may stray from
the external world to foolishly lose itself in introspec-
tions. Thoughts will come which suggest that the
soul is a mystic, and that the mind itself is a sphinx,
proposing riddles which no one can solve. This inspires respect, and reflection, and seriousness, and
leads to the border of religion. Whence? What?
Whither? Is there aught lurking behind the visible?
Is there no reason in the universe? Is there no grand
consummation? To be or not to be, that's the question. But he answers triumphantly: Man is a developed brute, the brute is developed matter, and matter
is developed atoms.

It is natural that the spiritual religion of scientific
materialism should no more be adapted to the thought-
less rabble than is its sublime morality; but there is
strong reason for the faith that by means of practical
materialism they will be trained to appreciate this religion. At present their downright honesty is perversity itself. When they get hold of a principle they
carry it to its ultimate conclusions, regardless of propriety or consequences; and by hasty applications,
which a cultured man carefully avoids, they pervert
the most salutary system ever devised. Unfortunately,
they see the value of a religion only in its application,
not in its mere conceptions and ideals. As soon as
science demonstrates that there is no personal God,
but that atoms are the deity, the masses speak of materialism as godless. But the shrewd materialist
speaks of nature, or law, or the beautiful order of

the universe, or something else as God, and thus indignantly refutes the base charge of godlessness. The ordinary man does not find his soul deeply agitated by awe and reverence at the thought of a universe devoid of reason and will, but governed by blind law ; the materialist, however, becomes eloquent over the awe-inspiring conceptions of such a cosmos ; and where common-sense can see nothing to adore in a force that can no more help itself than it can know that it works, he will be reverential and devout, and will worship, even if it must be himself. Where the narrow understanding can find no trace of religion, the broad one scents it even in atheism. Thus the religion which exerts the utmost restraint over materialists might lead the common herd to boundless licentiousness.

The materialist knows that death ends all ; but this constrains him to become an 'optimist, and impels him to make life sublime and worthy of its glorious destiny. But if an ordinary man is once convinced that the hope of a personal immortality is a farce, he actually lives as if the present life were the all of his being, and does not care if the devil does get what is left of him after all is destroyed. Live for posterity ? That depends on his social instincts, whether they are exerted for the future or not. On the principle of utilitarian ethics : What has posterity done for him to claim his gratitude ? And with his perverted logic and incurable stupidity, he is inclined to treat others, as well as himself, as if they were only developed brutes ; as if there were no God, no eternal life ; and as if men were destined to rot. And the fool becomes a pessimist ! These fellows accumulate wealth, build palaces, beautify their grounds, adorn their persons ; and then, instead of philosophic contentment, they yield to sentimental reflections, and sometimes it seems as if the Book of Ecclesiastes had addled their brains.   Melancholy brooding suggests that their wealth cannot be theirs forever ; that some prodigal may speedily waste what they have spent a life in anxiously accumulating ; that the palaces will remain after they are gone, and within will be feasting and music and dancing after they are forgotten ; and that the grounds which their hands have beautified will echo to the footsteps of strangers long, long after they have been silent in death.   As life folds up year after year in its bosom, they realize the more deeply that every road leads to death, and there ends.   Life is a growth in dreariness in proportion as it grows in culture, increase of refinement and sensitiveness being a development in misery.   Friend, parent, wife, child —all that are loved are committed to the tomb ; and with broken health and broken heart the old man totters to his grave—his life a memory, without a ray of hope, save that death will soon annihilate him too ; and he meets his doom in despair.   Instead of bearing up like a man and hero, he behaves like a baby ! Not a few end in suicide.   Poor sentimentalists ! That they must still have souls after it has been demonstrated that there is nothing but matter.

These dupes cannot understand why the atoms developed such a spirit in man, and then let him perish. They have learned to regard their aspirations and inspirations as the greatest blessing, but they prove to be the deepest curse.   Man knows that he must die, and this knowledge is his prerogative over the animal ; he abhors death, and this proves his nobleness ; and the climax of his glory is reached when he dies with a misery for which no animal has a capacity. The ignorant fellow does not see how endowments could originate which were never intended to be satisfied ; how there can be a capacity to which nothing is adapted ; and he imagines that this may even conflict with the law of the conservation of energy. Is not that force wasted, he asks, which spends itself in making man's highest faculties and then leaves them, not only absolutely useless, but actually without a sphere in which they can exert themselves ? Is it any wonder that in his ignorance he curses the power which gave him the intensest desire for happiness only to make his disappointment and misery infinite ? Poor fellow ! He forgets that there is nothing to swear by ; that in a universe without heart, and reason, and conscience, and mercy, and justice, as well as without eye and ear, a man cannot even have the poor satisfaction of giving vent to his feelings through an oath !

The spiritual materialist simply laughs at the ravings of these heart-broken sentimentalists. He soars above the clouds and basks in eternal sunshine. Man's capacity for virtue and enjoyment, his spiritual nature, with its pantings and aspirings, his cheering faith and inspiring hope, and his intense, agonizing efforts to free himself from nature's bondage, are simply intended (so far as matter intends at all) to create a sphere for poetry and romance, without which this life would be intolerably dull. They make genius possible, and give impulse to the creative powers ; they have evolved the most sublime conceptions which ever stirred human hearts ; they have kindled eloquence, and have incited to all that is highest in art ;

they inspired the sacred books of the East on which
the Oriental religions were founded ; and they gave
birth to all that is noble in man and grand in history.
So far from being useless, these gifts of the intellect
and heart are man's glory, and the crowning work of
the atoms. And that man in whom matter has
evolved and transmuted itself into endowments which
constitute all that can be called divine in the universe
is an ingrate wretch if he does not cheerfully perish
and thankfully rot like his kin, the brutes.

Having now followed materialism from the atoms
to religion, I shall close this work on science by hold-
ing up to the scorn of my fellow modern scientists
the words uttered by the President of the British Association, at Montreal : " Many excellent people are
afraid of science as tending toward materialism. That
such apprehension should exist is not surprising, for
unfortunately there are writers, speaking in the name
of science, who have set themselves to foster it. It
is true that among scientific men, as in other classes,
crude views are to be met with as to the deeper things
of nature ; but that the life-long beliefs of Newton,
of Faraday, and of Maxwell are inconsistent with the
scientific habit of mind, is surely a proposition which
I need not pause to refute."

www.ingramcontent.com/pod-product-compliance
Lightning Source LLC
Chambersburg PA
CBHW030840270326
41928CB00007B/1150